PHP Arrays

Single, Multi-dimensional, Associative
and Object Arrays in PHP 7

Steve Prettyman

Apress®

PHP Arrays: Single, Multi-dimensional, Associative and Object Arrays in PHP 7

Steve Prettyman
Key West, Florida, USA

ISBN-13 (pbk): 978-1-4842-2555-4   ISBN-13 (electronic): 978-1-4842-2556-1
DOI 10.1007/978-1-4842-2556-1

Library of Congress Control Number: 2016961720

Managing Director: Welmoed Spahr
Lead Editor: Steve Anglin
Technical Reviewer: Tri Phan
Editorial Board: Steve Anglin, Pramila Balan, Laura Berendson, Aaron Black, Louise Corrigan, Jonathan Gennick, Robert Hutchinson, Celestin Suresh John, Nikhil Karkal, James Markham, Susan McDermott, Matthew Moodie, Natalie Pao, Gwenan Spearing
Coordinating Editor: Mark Powers
Copy Editor: Brendan Frost
Compositor: SPi Global
Indexer: SPi Global
Artist: SPi Global
Cover image: Designed by Freepik

Distributed to the book trade worldwide by Springer Science+Business Media New York, 233 Spring Street, 6th Floor, New York, NY 10013. Phone 1-800-SPRINGER, fax (201) 348-4505, e-mail orders-ny@springer-sbm.com, or visit www.springeronline.com. Apress Media, LLC is a California LLC and the sole member (owner) is Springer Science + Business Media Finance Inc (SSBM Finance Inc). SSBM Finance Inc is a **Delaware** corporation.

For information on translations, please e-mail rights@apress.com, or visit www.apress.com.

Apress and friends of ED books may be purchased in bulk for academic, corporate, or promotional use. eBook versions and licenses are also available for most titles. For more information, reference our Special Bulk Sales–eBook Licensing web page at www.apress.com/bulk-sales.

Any source code or other supplementary materials referenced by the author in this text are available to readers at www.apress.com. For detailed information about how to locate your book's source code, go to www.apress.com/source-code/. Readers can also access source code at SpringerLink in the Supplementary Material section for each chapter.

Printed on acid-free paper

This book is dedicated to my wife, Beverly. Thank you for over 20 years of love and support; without you, this book would not be possible.

Contents at a Glance

Contents

About the Author

Steve Prettyman earned his bachelor of arts degree in education from Oglethorpe University in 1979. He quickly began his teaching career as a high school mathematics instructor while continuing his education by earning a master's degree in business information systems from Georgia State University (1985). Since then, Steve has spent over 30 years in the IT industry. The last, almost 20 years, he has been an instructor and professor at Chattahoochee Technical College, Kennesaw State University, and Southern Polytechnic State University. He is currently the Computer Science Department Chair for Florida Keys Community College, Key West, Florida. His primary teaching responsibilities include programming, web design, and web application development.

About the Technical Reviewer

Tri Phan is the founder of the Programming Learning Channel on YouTube. He has over seven years of experience in the software industry. Specifically, he has worked in many outsourcing companies and has written many applications of many fields in different programming languages such as PHP, Java, and C#. In addition, he has over six years of experience in teaching at international and technological centers such as Aptech, NIIT, and Kent College.

Introduction

PHP Arrays: Single, Multidimensional, Associative, and Object Arrays in PHP 7 is intended for use as a supplemental beginning-level programming book. It is not the goal of this book to cover advanced techniques in the current versions of the PHP programming language. Some beginning knowledge of general PHP programming concepts is expected but no actual programming experience or education is assumed.

All code examples in this book are compatible with PHP 7. The newest methods (functions) available in PHP have been used to provide the reader with the most current coding techniques. The examples use core methods provided in the PHP language. PHP includes many additional methods to accomplish similar tasks as shown within. The reader may, and should, research additional advanced array techniques after understanding the material presented in this book.

Special Note—Teachers

This book is provided as a supplementary guide to introductory textbooks on PHP 7. The intent of this book is to provide additional examples and explanation of the power and use of arrays in the PHP language. PHP arrays provide many capabilities that arrays in other languages do not provide.

Teaching tools, including test banks, course outline, and PowerPoint slides are available as part of the source code download available at the Apress website.

Code Examples, Images, and Links

Every effort has been made to catch any errors in code (and grammar). Please let us know if/when you discover problems in this book. Please send all corrections to Steve Prettyman (steve_prettyman@hotmail.com).

All code examples, images, and links are available for download from the following location. Please download code examples from the website. Copying code from the book may cause errors due to format requirements for publishing.

www.apress.com/9781484225554

CHAPTER 1

■ ■ ■

PHP 7 Basics

After completing this chapter, the student will be able to...

Create a simple error-free PHP program

Understand the use and value of conditional statements

Understand the use and value of for, while, and foreach loops

Understand the use and value of functions

Understand the use and value of arrays

Understand the basic structure of an object-oriented PHP program

1.1   Installation

The PHP environment can be installed on almost any operating system. This allows the developer the ability to easily create a development and testing environment. Complete testing can and should be completed before the code is installed in a live environment. The developer should determine the major PHP version used in the live environment and replicate this same version in the test environment.

PHP 7 includes many new tools and has removed some tools from previous versions. Therefore, it is imperative that both the live environment and the testing environment be the same. The testing environment can also be used to test minor release changes on existing code before the live environment is upgraded to the new release.

Although PHP can be installed by itself, novice and less experienced programmers should use one of the many installation tools available to install PHP with Apache Server, MySQL, PhpAdmin, and other related applications. These packages greatly simplify the process and are free and open source. Installing PHP separately requires a more in-depth knowledge of what versions of tools are compatible and changes required to the configuration files to link these tools together.

Apache, which is open source and free, is the most common server to use with PHP. However, PHP can be used with other servers, including Microsoft's Web Server. It is beyond the scope of this book to look at other servers. However, you can find installation information on the Internet.

Electronic supplementary material The online version of this chapter (doi:10.1007/978-1-4842-2556-1_1) contains supplementary material, which is available to authorized users.

MySQL, which is also open source and free, is the most common database used with PHP. PHP has the ability to use other databases, including Oracle and SQL Server among others. In many cases, the coding used to manipulate MySQL databases is very similar to the code used to manipulate other databases. php. net includes some basic information on drivers and coding for non-MySQL databases. You can also find additional information on the database's websites. PhpAdmin is a free tool to easily create and update MySQL database information. As stated before, most packages include a version of this software.

LAMP (Linux, Apache, MySQL, PHP), MAMP (Mac, Apache, MySQL, PHP), and WAMP (Windows, Apache, MySQL, PHP) package versions are readily available on the web. There are many organizations that currently create similar packages. We will briefly look at one of them. However, you will find that they all work in a similar way.

1.2 EasyPhp

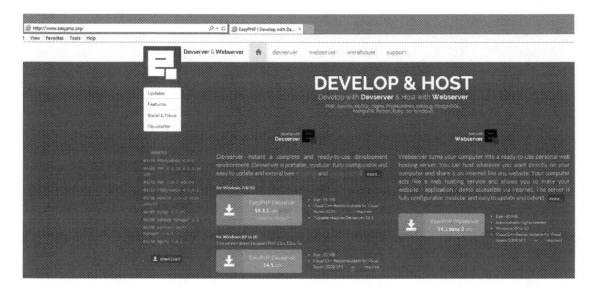

Figure 1-1. *EasyPhp*

The EasyPhp Development Server (available at easyphp.net) is a WAMP package which includes many additional tools, including the following:

Python

Ruby

Perl

Nginx

You can install this package on any storage device, including a usb key, memory stick, external hard drive, or your internal hard drive. This package provides easy configurations, along with direct access to your applications and files. In addition to configuration files, error logs, access logs, and application logs are provided. Additional features can be added to the base installation. Some of these are provided on the EasyPhp website.

1.2.1   Installing EasyPhp

The first time you attempt to install the development sever, you should accept the default settings provided by the developers. If you run into problems during installation, review the "Resolving Problems" section of this chapter.

▓ **Warning**   Pay attention to what buttons you are clicking when downloading the software. You might install much more than just EasyPhp.

1.2.2   Resolving Problems

The following are some of the most common installation problems and resolutions to these problems. If you encounter a problem not shown, or the resolution shown does not work in your environment, copy and paste any error code you receive in a search engine (such as Google) to determine how others have solved the problem.

1.2.3   Missing C# Library

PHP 7 and earlier versions of PHP require the Microsoft Visual Studio C# library. If you have Windows 8/10, this library is probably already installed. Also, if you have a recent version of Microsoft Visual Studio, it is also probably already installed. If you receive an error indicating that C# is missing or the wrong version, paste the message into a search engine on the Internet. Search for a response from Microsoft for directions to fix the error. The response should include a link to download the missing files and installation instructions.

1.2.4   Port Conflicts

If you already have a service using port 80, the default port for HTML traffic between your PC and the outside world, you will receive an error message from Apache when it attempts to run. You can fix this problem in multiple ways.

A. If you don't mind shutting down other services using the port while you are developing, you can follow the next directions. Once you are done using Apache and PHP, you can turn the services back on or just reboot your PC and the services will turn back on.

1. Go to the Microsoft Windows 7/8/10 Task Manager (press Ctrl+Alt+Delete at the same time).

2. Select the Services tab.

3. Look for any of the following services in Windows 7/8/10. If you find one running, right-click it and turn it off. Then try restarting Apache again. If that does not work, turn that one back on and try another one. (The names may be slightly different depending on the version of Windows.)

SQL Server Reporter, Web Deployment Agent, BranchCache, Sync Share Service, WAS (IIS Administrator), and W3SVC

B. If you need your other services running or you do not have the administrative privileges to turn off services on port 80, you can change the default listening port location for Apache.

Go to your system tray (bottom-right corner of your screen). Find the EasyPHP icon by scrolling over the icons. A description of each should appear. If you don't see the icon, click the up arrow in the system tray to see more icons. Right-click the EasyPHP icon. Select Configuration and then select Apache. This will open the Apache configuration file (httpd.conf) into Notepad (or your default text editor). First save a copy of this file somewhere in case you make an error. This will allow you to recover from any major mistakes that occur.

Search for "Listen 127.0.0.1:80" within the file. Change the occurrence of 80 to 8080 or to 81; on that line only. This will allow the Apache server to listen to one of the ports that are not commonly used. Resave the file (make sure you are resaving the original file to the original location).

▓ **Note**   Make sure when you're using Notepad or any other text editor that you use Save As, and then select All Files for the file type. Also make sure to include the .conf file extension. If you do not change the file type to all files, your file will be saved as httpd.conf.txt. If that happens, the server will not see the file. You can easily fix the problem by reopening the file and saving it in the proper method.

You can then restart Apache by going back to your system tray to find the EasyPHP icon. Double-click the icon; a message box will appear that will give you the status Apache and MySQL. You will probably see red for the Apache status. Click the Apache button. Within a few moments, it should turn green. This will indicate that the server is now running. Do the same for MySQL.

1.2.5   Missing Files

If you receive an error message related to this, somehow your files have become corrupted before installation. Return to the EasyPHP web site and download the files again. Also, if you somehow mess up the Apache configuration file, go back and reinstall the product again.

1.2.6   Can't Install Files in Program Files Directory

This indicates that you or something else has a high security restriction on that directory. Rerun the installation and change the location of your installation to another directory. Just remember when we reference the program files directory later in this book that you should instead look at the directory in which your files were installed.

1.2.7   Apache Delays and Hang-ups

In Windows 8/10 you may experience problems with Apache working slowly or hanging up. To correct this problem go to your system tray (bottom-right corner of your screen). Find the EasyPHP icon by scrolling over the icons. A description of each should appear. If you don't see the icon, click the up arrow in the system tray to see more icons. Right-click the EasyPHP icon. Select Configuration and then select Apache.

This will open the Apache configuration file (httpd.conf) into Notepad (or your default text editor). First save a copy of this file somewhere in case you make an error. This will allow you to recover from any major mistakes that occur.

Then add the following two lines to the bottom of the file.

AcceptFilter http none

AcceptFilter https none

Resave the file (make sure you are resaving the original file to the original location).

1.3   Testing Your Environment

Before spending a lot of time coding, you need to ensure that your environment has been set up properly. The following suggestions will provide some clues to indicate if the environment is working.

1. Testing Your Administration Environment

   First we need to test the server and see if our administration pages will display. Open your favorite browser and enter the following: `http://127.0.0.1/home/`

   If the environment is working, you will see an administrative page for Apache Server. Otherwise, check to see if the server is actually running in your computer's services tab.

2. Testing the Development Environment

   Open a text editor (such as Notepad, Notepad++, or Textedit) and enter the following code:

   ```
   <?php
       print "Hello World";
   ?>
   ```

Using the *Save As* selection on the File menu, change the File Type to *All Files* or to *php*. Enter the file name test.php and save it to the following location.

```
C:\Program Files (x86)\EasyPHP-DevServer-16.1VC11\data\localweb\projects
```

Of course, you should change the version name (or program file name) to the correct version (location) that you are using on your machine.

If you saved your files correctly, you can attempt to run your program by entering the following in your browser.

```
http://127.0.0.1/projects/test.php
```

1.3.1   Resolving Problems

If "Hello World" does not display in your browser when you run the test program, review the following error resolutions. If you do not see your error, or the suggested resolution does not work, copy and paste your error message into a browser and try some of the suggestions from other users on the web.

Nothing is displayed, error 404:

1. Make sure you typed the address exactly as shown.

2. Your server might be hung up. Stop and restart it.

3. Make sure you placed your file in the correct location.

4. Make sure you saved your file as a .php file and not as .txt. Try *Save As* again and renaming the file (make sure file type is either All Files or php).

5. Check for typos in your actual program code. Did you remember the semicolon (;)?

   Fix any and resave. You might need to stop and start the server if it does not see the changes for some reason. You can go look at the PHP log files to see any errors that might exist in your code.

6. Go to the Apache log files to look for errors. If you cannot correct them, copy the errors and paste them in a search engine to see what others have found as solutions.

The actual program code is displayed not the results of executing the code:

1. Make sure you saved your file as a .php file and not as .txt. Try Save As again and renaming the file (make sure file type is either All Files or php).

2. Your Apache server or PHP might not be started or is hung. Stop and start Apache again.

3. Did you forget or have a typo in the *<?php* or *?>* lines?

4. Go to the Apache log files to find the errors. If you cannot correct them, copy the errors and paste them in a search engine to see what others have found as solutions.

1.4 Alias Directories

Apache allows you to create additional directories to host your PHP programs. Alias directories must include an alias name (such php1) and the actual physical location of the file(s) (such as c://myfiles/php). The alias name is used by the server to determine the actual location of the file.

`www.nothingmuch.com/php1/test.php`

The user entering this address might assume that the test.php program exists in a folder with a name of php1. However, this might not be the case. If php1 is actually an alias directory the browser will redirect to a different location (such as c://myfiles). This feature allows some sense of security because the user does not know which files are kept where. It also allows flexibility as files could be moved (from c://myfiles) to another location (such as c://oldfiles) without the user knowing. The person moving the files can update the alias information in the server to a new location, and keep the same alias name (such as php1).

1.5 How It All Works

When a url is entered into a browser, the request is sent to a web server (Apache). If the file contains only html, JavaScript, and/or css, then the file requested is sent directly to the requesting browser. The requesting browser will then interpret the html, css, and JavaScript code. The results of the interpretation are then displayed in the browser.

If the file contains additional code, such as PHP, the server (Apache) will determine how to handle the additional code. PHP programs run within the Apache server (not the browser). The Apache server uses the file ending (.php) to determine if there is PHP code within a file. It will use the opening (<?php) and closing (?>) tags that surround PHP code to determine what needs to be sent to the PHP environment to be interpreted and executed. The PHP environment will return the results of the execution of the program, such as "Hello World" in the test example, back to the Apache server. The server will then return any output (along with any html, css, and/or JavaScript code) back to the browser.

PHP code can be mixed with html, css, and JavaScript.

```
<html>
<head><title>Hello World</title></head>
<body>
<?php
    print "Hello World";
?>
</body>
</html>
```

The test PHP program shown previously could include html code as shown in the preceding. The output seen by the user would not change. However, the preceding html would exist within the browser window.

```
<html>
<head><title>Hello World</title></head>
<body>
        Hello World
</body>
</html>
```

If you view the source code resulting from the execution of the last example (right-click, view source), you will see the html code that did not exist within the test program (as shown in the preceding).

In this example, the html code will be interpreted by the browser. The PHP code will be sent to the Apache server to be processed. The Apache server will send the code to the PHP environment for processing. The PHP environment will interpret the code and send the results back to the Apache server. The results of the interpretation of the code will be returned to the browser.

PHP programs can also output html code when executed.

```
<html>
<head><title>Hello World</title></head>
<body>
<?php
    print "<h1>Hello World</h1>";
?>
</body>
</html>
```

In this example, everything within the quotes in the PHP statement will be sent back to the Apache Server (along with the html code shown). This would include the h1 statements shown. All the code returned to the Apache sever would then be sent back to the browser. The browser would then interpret all code returned (which includes all the html statements, the h1 tags, and the "Hello World" string). The browser will display "Hello World" as a header on the web page.

1.6   Editors

PHP programs do not require any special IDEs or editors to create code. Since PHP code is not compiled, the server will interpret the code when it is executed. This allows the developer the ability to use any text editor (such as Notepad or Notepad++). The developer must ensure that all file endings containing PHP code include .php. By default, Notepad and other text editors use .txt as a file ending. By using "save as" in the file menu of the editor, the developer can adjust the file ending to ".php." As mentioned earlier, if the code is not interpreted by the server, check the file ending. Many times the txt file endings are hidden. Thus, if you are not careful, a file ending like ".php.txt" could be created. In many cases, code contained in this file would not execute. This could easily be fixed by going back into the editor and resaving the file in the proper format.

There are many free editors available that can be used to write PHP code. One of the most popular is Notepad++ (notpad-plus-plus.org). You can find additional free editors at download.com.

1.7   The Basic Syntax

Now let's do a quick review of some of the basic components of the PHP language. If you find difficulty with any of the following topics, you may want to review many of the free videos and tutorials on the Web, including thenewboston.com and w3cschools.com.

```php
<?php
    // code goes here
?>
```

As stated earlier, all PHP code must be placed between the <?php and ?> tags. Comments can be created using // (as shown in the preceding).

```php
<?php
    print "Hello World";
?>
```

All executable code must include a semicolon at the end of the statement. Any strings (such as Hello World in the preceding) must be included in either double "" or single '' marks. Some PHP functions require the use of one or the other. All PHP functions begin with a lowercase letter (as in print). Most functions usually accept parameters that are passed into the function. In this example, the string "Hello World" is passed into the print function.

```php
<?php
    myFunction("Hello World");
?>
```

Most functions require () around the attributes that are passed into the function.

```php
<?php
    $result = addIt(12, 13);
    print $result;
?>
```

Variables store information in memory. In PHP you do not need to declare a data type when using a variable. You actually don't even need to declare a variable separately before using it. In the preceding example, a variable ($result) will hold whatever is returned by a function called addIt. This function accepts two parameters (12, 13), which we assume will add the numbers together and return the result. The print statement will then display whatever is contained in the variable.

When declaring variables or functions, the developer can use many styles. The most common is camel case. In camel case the first word is lowercase and the remaining words have a capitalized first letter, such as addIt. However, other styles are acceptable, such as:

```
$first_number
$second_Number
$_value
```

Variables must always include the $ as the first character, and alphabetic characters. They can also include the underscore (_). No other special symbols are allowed. No spaces are allowed.

```
1:  $myValue = "Help";
2:  $myValue = 123;
3:  $myValue = 123 + 456;
4:  $myValue = "Help" . " me!";
5:  $myValue = "Help " . 123;
```

The data type is determined the first time a variable is used.

1. The data type is string (characters).

2. The data type would change to integer (whole numbers).

3. 123 and 456 are added together and the result is placed into the variable (which now holds an integer).

4. This statement uses the string concatenation character (.) to merge the two strings together to form "Help me!" which is then placed in the variable (which—you guessed it—now contains a string).

5. This statement merges a string and integer. PHP will convert the integer to a string "123" to allow it to be concatenated with the other string to produce "Help 123," which will be placed into the variable.

Mathematics

Operator	Example	Description	Similar Operation
+	$num = 1 + 2;	Add	
~	$num = 1 − 2;	Subtract	
*	$num = 1 * 2;	Multiply	
/	$num = 1 / 2;	Divide	
%	$num = 1 % 2;	Modular/Remainder	
++	++$num; $num++;	Increment	$num = $num + 1;
~~	--$num; $num--;	Decrement	$num = $num − 1;

Arithmetic operations work in a similar way to mathematics. The exception is that the calculation is done on the right side of the expression (right side of the = sign) and the result is placed into the variable (or other object) on the left side of the expression ($num). PHP includes many functions to produce results seen on a calculator (for more information visit php.net). PHP also allows you to use parentheses () to change the order in which values are calculated. Otherwise the language follows the normal mathematical order of operations.

Variables can be incremented/decremented before they are used (++$num, --$num), or after they are used ($num++, $num--).

Assignment Operators

	Operator	Example	Similar Operation
1:	=	$my_num = 1;	
2:	+=	$my_num += 1;	$my_num = $my_num + 1;
3:	-=	$my_num -= 1;	$my_num = $my_num -1;
4:	*=	$my_num *= 1;	$my_num = $my_num * 1;
5:	/=	$my_num /= 1;	$my_num = $my_num / 1;
6:	%=	$my_num %= 2;	$my_num = $my_num % 2;
7:	.=	$my_value .= "Hi";	$my_value = $my_value . "Hi";

1. The assignment operator (=) will take the value from the right side of the expression (1) and place it into the variable ($my_num) on the left side of the expression. If the variable does not exist, it will be created in memory. The data type (in this case integer) will be determined when the value is placed in the variable.

2. This statement adds the value on the right side of the expression (1) to the contents (value) that exists in the variable ($my_num) on the left side of the expression. If the variable has not existed before, zero will be added to the value on the right side and the result is placed into the variable ($my_num). If a string exists in the variable, an attempt will be made to convert it to a number.

3. This statement is similar to #2, except the value on the right side is subtracted from the value contained in the variable. If the variable did not previously exist, the value on the right side (1) is subtracted from 0. In this example, 1 will be subtracted from the value in $my_num and the result will be placed back into $my_num. If a string exists in the variable, an attempt will be made to convert it to a number.

4. This statement is similar to #3, except the value is multiplied instead of added. If the variable did not previously exist, the value on the right side (1) is multiplied by 0. If a string exists in the variable, an attempt will be made to convert it to a number.

5. This statement is similar to #4, except the value from the right side is divided into the value contained in the variable. Only the integer result (whole number) is placed into the variable. If a string exists in the variable, an attempt will be made to convert it to a number.

6. This statement is similar to #5, except the remainder of the division is placed into the variable. If a string exists in the variable, an attempt will be made to convert it to a number.

7. The period (.) is the string concatenation symbol. In this example "Hi" is added to whatever string exists within the variable ($my_value). If the variable has not existed previously, then the variable is assumed to hold an empty string. If a numeric value is contained in the variable, an attempt will be made to convert it to a string. Then the string given ("Hi") will be concatenated to it.

Comparison Operators

	Operation Result	returns TRUE if...
1:	$a == $b	$a and $b are equal ignoring cases
2:	$a === $b	$a and $b equal if case is the same
3:	$a != $b, $a <> $b	$a and $b are not equal ignoring cases
4:	$a !== $b	$a and $b are not equal or not same case
5:	$a < $b	$a is less than $b
6:	$a <= $b	$a is less than or equal to $b
7:	$a > $b	$a is greater than $b
8:	$a >= $b	$a is greater than or equal to $b
9:	$a <=> $b	returns -1 if $a < b, returns 0 if $a equals $b, returns 1 if $a > $b

Comparing two values to determine if they are equal requires two (==) or three (===) equal signs. One (=) equal sign is used as an "assignment operator" as shown in the last table.

1.8 Conditional Statements

Conditional statements determine if a comparison is "true" or "false." If the statement is true, then the code right after the if statement is executed. If the statement is false, the code after the else statement (if there is one) is executed.

Examples using conditional statements with comparison operators:

1.

```php
<?php
        $a = 25; $b = 36;

        if( $a == $b) {
                print "$b equals $a";
        }
        else {
                print "$b and $a are not equal";
}
?>
```

25 and 36 are not equal

PHP will interpret $b and $a within the string and output the contents of each as shown in the preceding.

2.

```php
<?php
        $a = "a"; $b = "b";
        if( $a === $b) {
                print "$b equals $a";
        }
        else {
                print "$b and $a are not equal";
        }
?>
```

A and a are not equal

Using three equal signs (===) also compares case. In this example the comparison is false due to the case. If you remove one of the equal signs, the result would be true.

3.

```php
<?php
        $a = 25; $b = 36;
        if( $a != $b) {
                print "$b and $a are not equal";
        else {
                print "$b and $a are not equal";
        }
?>
```

25 and 36 are not equal

The not operator works in reverse of the equals operator (see #1).

4.

```php
<?php
        $a = "A"; $b = "a";
        if( $a !== $b) {
                print "$b and $a are not equal";
        }
        else {
                print "$b and $a are equal";
        }
?>
```

a and A are not equal.

The not case operator works in reverse of the case operator (see #2).

5.

```php
<?php
        $a = 25; $b = 36;
        if( $a < $b) {
                print "$a is less than $b";
        }
        else {
                print "$b is greater than $a";
        }
?>
```

25 is less than 36

Less than returns true if the value on the left is less than the value on the right.

6.

```php
<?php
        $a = 36; $b = 36;
        if( $a <= $b) {
                print "$a is less than or equal to $b";
        }
        else {
                print "$b is greater than $a";
        }
?>
```

36 is less than or equal to 36

The less than or equal to comparison works similar to #5. However, if the values are equal then it returns true.

7.

```php
<?php
        $a = 25; $b = 36;
        if( $a > $b) {
                print "$a is greater than $b";
        }
        else {
                print "$b is greater than $a";
        }
?>
```

36 is greater than 25

The greater than comparison returns true if the left value is greater than the right value.

8.

```php
<?php
        $a = 36; $b = 36;
        if( $a >= $b) {
                print "$a is greater than or equal to $b";
        }
        else {
                print "$b is greater than $a";
        }
?>
```

36 is greater than or equal to 36

The greater than or equal to comparison works similar to #7. However, if the two values are equal it returns true.

9.

```php
<?php
        $a = 36; $b = 36;
        $result = $a <=> $b;
        if( $result === 0) {
                print "Both are equal";
        } else if( $result === 1) {
                print "$a is greater than $b";
        } else {
                print "$b is greater than $a";
        }
?>
```

Both are equal

The rocket ship operator (available in PHP7+) returns –1 if $a < b, returns 0 if $a equals $b, or returns 1 if $a > $b.

Logical Operators

	Operator	returns TRUE if...
1:	AND, &&	both operands (sides of the expression) are "true"
2:	OR, ||	either operand (side of the expression) is "true"
3:	XOR	If and only if just one operand is "true"
4:	NOT !	Reverses the result (true -> false, false -> true)

Logical operators allow you to ask more than one question in a conditional statement. Examples:

1.

```php
<?php
        $a = 25; $b = 25; $c = 25; $d = 35;
        If ( $a == $b AND $c == $d ) {
                print "Everyone is equal!";
        } else {
                print "Someone is not equal";
        }
?>
```

Everyone is equal.

2.

```php
<?php
        $a = 25; $b = 25; $c = 35; $d = 35;
        If ( $a == $b OR $c == $d ) {
                print "Some or all of us are equal!";
        } else {
                print "No one is equal";
        }
?>
```

Some or all of us are equal.

Only one side of the comparison has to be true for the complete expression to be true.

3.

```php
<?php
        $a = 25; $b = 25; $c = 25; $d = 25;
        If ( $a == $b XOR $c == $d ) {
                print "Everyone is equal!";
        } else {
                print "Someone is not equal";
        }
?>
```

15

Someone is not equal

With excusive or (XOR) only one side of the expression can be true. In this example, both sides were true so it evaluates to false.

4.

```php
<?php
        $a = 25; $b = 25; $c = 25; $d = 25;
        If ( NOT ($a == $b XOR $c == $d ) ) {
                print "Everyone is equal!";
        } else {
                print "Someone is not equal";
        }
?>
```

Everyone is equal

The not expression reverses the result. This excusive or (XOR) returned false. However, the NOT reversed the result to true.

? Operator

The ? operator is a short coding version of a conditional if-then-else statement.

```php
<?php
        $a = 36; $b = 36;
        print $a = $b ? "They are equal" : "They are not equal";
?>
```

They are equal

The statement placed between the ? and : is executed if the comparison is true. The statement between the : and ; is executed if the statement is false. Since a print command is to the left of the comparison, the result of the comparison will be printed.

```php
<?php
        $a = 36; $b = 24;
        print $a <=> $b ? "They are equal" :
                "$a is greater than $b" :
                "$b is greater than $a";
?>
```

36 is greater than 24

In PHP 7+ you can also evaluate for 0, –1, and 1. This comparison becomes a very short and efficient determination of whether the values are equal, or which is greater.

1.9   Switch Statement

The switch statement can be used to eliminate embedded if-then-else statements which are determining a value within a variable.

```php
<?php
        $a = 36;
        switch ($a) {
                case 10:
                        print "10";
                        break;
                case 20:
                        print "20";
                        break;
                case 30:
                        print "30";
                        break;
                default:
                        print "Number was not found";
                break;
        }

?>
```

Number was not found

The break statement is required for each collection of expressions. In this example, the values in $a are compared to 10, 20, and 30. Since none of these comparisons is 'true' the code will execute the default section, which is similar to an else.

1.10   Functions

In addition to the thousands of built-in or easily importable PHP functions available for your use, you can also create your own functions.

```php
function function_name(atribute1, atribute2, ...) {

// code goes here

}
```

The general format of a function is shown in the preceding. The function keyword is lowercase. The name you provide for the function uses almost the same format at variables, except you do not include the $. Variables can be passed into the function in the parentheses. All code goes between the brackets {}.

```php
function display_hello() {
        print "Hello";
}
```

17

To call a function you use the function name and pass any required variables. In the preceding example no required variables are needed.

```php
<?php
    function display_hello() {
        print "Hello";
    }
    display_hello();
    }
?>
```

This code would display "Hello." The function can also be placed at the bottom of the code. However, be consistent. Place your functions either at the top or at the bottom of the code.

```php
<?php
    function display_hello($value) {
        print $value;
    }
        display_hello("Hello");
    }
?>
```

This example accomplishes the same task. However, it allows some flexibility by letting the user pass the value to be displayed. Notice that the string was passed within the parentheses when the function was called. The string will drop into the variable $value (it determines where values go by the position they are passed). The print statement in the function then uses the variable $value to display the information. This function would actually display almost anything passed, even though it is called display_hello.

```php
<?php
    function display_names( $first_name, $last_name = "none") {
        print "Your first name is $first_name";
        if ($last_name != "none") {
            print "Your last name is $last_name";
        }
    }
    display_names("James");
    display_names("Jackie", "Jones");
?>
```

This display_names function accepts two values ($first_name, $last_name). However, it also provides a default value for the second parameter. In the first call to the function, "James" will pass into $first_name. Since there is not a second parameter passed, $last_name will contain "none." "James" will be displayed. The if statement will determine that a second value has not been passed and will not attempt to display $last_name. In the second call, both values are passed. "Jackie" will be passed into $first_name. "Jones" will be passed into $last_name. The function will display "Jackie Jones."

```php
<?php
    function addtwo( $first_value, $second_value) {
        $result = $first_value +$second_value;
```

```
        return $result;
    }
    print addtwo( 12, 14);
?>
```

In the addtwo example, two numerical values are passed into the function. The call to the function causes 12 to be passed into $first_value and 14 to be placed into $second_value. The two numbers are added together and the result is place into $result. A return statement returns the value back to the program that called it (instead of displaying it). This allows the calling code the flexibility to determine what to do with the returned value. In this example, the function was called within a print execution. This will cause the value returned by the addtwo function (26) to be displayed.

```
<?php
    declare(strict_types=1);
    function addtwo( integer $first_value,integer $second_value) : integer {
        $result = $first_value +$second_value;
        return $result;
    }
    print addtwo( 12, 14);
?>
```

In PHP 7+ we can add *Scalar type hints* to restrict the type of information passed into and out of a function. In the preceding example, the parameters pass in are restricted to integers only as indicated by the integer keyword before the variable names. The return value is also restricted to integer, as indicated by the : integer as part of the function header. strict_type must be set to 1 for enforcement. If it is set to zero (the default) the data types shown will be ignored. Currently integer, string, bool, and float are the only valid data types.

include, include_once, require, require_once

As you develop functions you will discover that some could be used in multiple applications. These functions can reside in a separate file and be imported into an application.

```
<?php
    declare(strict_types=1);
    function addtwo( integer $first_value, integer $second_value) : integer {
        $result = $first_value + $second_value;
        return $result;
    }
?>
```

Functions that reside within their own files must still include the opening and closing php tags as shown in the preceding.

```
<?php
    include "addtwo.php";
    print addtwo( 12, 14);
?>
```

19

This program will import the addtwo.php file (which contains the addtwo function). Once it is imported, it can call the function as shown.

The include keyword will search for the file and attempt to include it in the program. If the file does not exist, the program will continue. The include_once keyword is similar to the include. However, it makes an additional check to discover if the file has already been imported. If it has, it ignores the request (does not produce an error). include would produce errors if the file has already been imported because there would now be multiple functions with the same name.

The require keyword is similar to the include keyword. However, if the file does not exist, an error will be produced. The require_once keyword is similar to the require keyword with the additional check to not load the file if it has already been loaded.

1.11   Try/Catch Blocks

The examples shown do not attempt to handle any errors. There are multiple possible problems with these examples, if the user does not enter what it expected. We can adjust the calling program to handle possible problems.

```php
<?php
    try {
            include "addtwo.php";
            print dividetwo( 12, 14);
    }
    catch(zeroException $e) {
            print "Don't try to divide by zero!";
    }
    catch(Exception $e) {
            print $e->getMessage();
    }
    catch(Error $e) {
            print $e->getMessage();
    }
?>
```

In this example, both the include statement and the print statement are placed in a try block. The program will execute statements in a try block until it runs into a problem. When a problem occurs it will look for a catch block to handle the problem. Since the include statement depends on a file existing external to the program, it is important that the program be able to handle the possibility that the file might not exist. This example also places the dividetwo function within the try block. If this dividetwo function attempts to divide by zero, PHP will raise an exception.

Starting with PHP 7+ all Exceptions and Errors can be handled within the program. In this example, the code specially captures the zeroException exception which would be raised by PHP if an attempt was made to divide by zero. If that occurs, the message shown in the block would be displayed and the program would shut down properly (not error).

In addition, two additional catch blocks are shown. The second catch captures all other *Exceptions* caused by the program. The third catch block captures all *Errors*, including syntax errors. If the execution of the code jumps the flow into one of these blocks, the standard error message would be displayed and the program would be shut down without crashing. It is important to ensure that live programs do not crash. It is better to capture any problems and then display a message to the user requesting that they try using the system again later.

1.12   Arrays

Arrays hold multiple related information in memory. For example, an array might contain class information such as class number, class name, description, room, instructor, and size (number of students).

```
$class_array[0] = "CS122";
// class number
$class_array[1] ="Programming Concepts 1";
// class name
$class_array[2] ="Basic concepts of the PHP language.";
// description
$class_array[3] = "B123"; // room
$class_array[4] = "Dr. Abraham Excell";
// instructor
$class_array[5] = 50;
// number of students
```

This array has been created dynamically (on the fly). We can also create the array using a more common format.

```
$class_array = array ( 'CS122',
        'Programming Concepts 1',
        'Basic concepts of the PHP language.',
        'B123', 'Dr. Abraham Excell', 50);
```

This format will also create the array, using fewer lines of code. The array itself actually behaves in exactly the same way as the previous array. Both of these arrays require us to remember what content is placed in which position. We can use *Associate Arrays* to name our positions (subscripts) instead of using numbers.

```
$class_array["class number"] = "CS122";
$class_array["class name"] ="Programming Concepts 1";
$class_array["description"] ="Basic concepts of the PHP language.";
$class_array["room"] = "B123";
$class_array["instructor"] ="Dr. Abraham Excell";
$class_array["number of students"] = 50;
```

This provides an easier-to-understand relationship between the values and the array. We can also create the same relationship with the other format shown to create an array.

```
$class_array = array (
        array ( 'CS122', 'Programming Concepts 1',
                'Basic concepts of the PHP language.',
                'B123', 'Dr. Abraham Excell', 50),
        array ( 'CS123', 'Programming Concepts 2',
                'Advanced concepts of the PHP language.',
                'B124', 'Dr. Abraham Excell', 50)
);
```

Arrays can also be multidimensional. The preceding array contains two rows representing two different classes. We will look at arrays in more detail in the coming chapters.

1.13   For, While, Foreach Loops

Loops provide the ability to execute the same code multiple times.

```
$I = 1;
while ($I <= 10) {
        print "$I times";
        $I++;
}
```

This block of code would produce 1 times 2 times 3 times 4 times 5 times 6 times 7 times 8 times 9 times 10 times.

The *for loop* works well when you know exactly how many times you want to loop. In the example, $I is set to 1. Then the loop iterates as long as $I is less than or equal to 10. Each time the loop reaches the top, the value of I is increased by 1.

```
$I = 1;
while ($I <= 10) {
        print "$I times";
        I++;
}
```

The same task can be accomplished with a *while loop*. However, as you can see, it does take slightly more code. You also have to remember to include the incrementing of the counting variable ($I++). If that statement is forgotten, the loop would become infinite. With the for loop, you are easily reminded to increment the variable in the top statement in the loop. While loops are good for conditions that might change, such as looping until you reach the end of a file or end of an array.

```
foreach( $class_array as $value)
{
        print $value;
}
```

foreach loops work well with arrays. The preceding example loops through the one-dimensional array ($class_array) shown previously and displays each value. $value represents the current value that the loop is looking at in the array. foreach loops do not require the programmer to create code that checks for the end of the array. This eliminates any possibility that an "Out of Bounds" error message could occur. Also, foreach loops automatically skip over any positions in the array that have not yet be declared. This eliminates any possible "Null value" messages being displayed when it loops through the array.

1.14   Classes, Properties, Objects

PHP is an *object-oriented language*. Object-oriented languages can declare *classes* that contain *properties* (variables) and *methods* (functions). One or more instances of a class (called an *Object*) can be declared and used within the program.

The use of classes and objects mimic the real world. In the animal kingdom, all animals have some similar characteristics, such as the eyes and eye color. These common characteristics (which we call properties in PHP) can be saved in a class called animals. Also common behaviors, such as movement (which would exist in methods) can be saved in the same animal class. Lions are (of course) a type of animal. As such, they inherit all the characteristics of an animal (they inherit the animal class). However, lions, themselves have similar characteristics and behaviors that define them as a lion. A lion class could inherit the animal class and include those unique traits that make a lion a lion. African lions are different than Asian lions. An African lion class (or Asian lion class) could, again, provide the differences. Finally, an actual lion living in Africa is an object which physically exists, inheriting from the African lion class, which inherits from the lion class, which inherits from the animal class.

Let's look at a simple example, to get a general understanding. If you are interested in a more in-depth understanding, there are many textbooks and free website tutorials/videos that can help enhance your studies.

```php
<?php
    class Lion {
        // code goes here
    }
?>
```

All properties (variables) and methods (functions) are contained within the brackets of the class as shown in the preceding. Classes are said to be *encapsulated* as the class provides a capsule to hold and protect everything within. We have already discovered that classes can use *inheritance* to pull in properties and methods from another class. Object-oriented languages also provide *polymorphism*, which allows methods and other objects to have the same name, but the ability to function differently. For example, several versions of an addnumber method could have different *signatures* which allow a different amount of numbers to be passed into the method to produce a sum of the values passed.

```php
<?php
class Lion {
    private $color = "no color";
    private $weight = 0;
}
?>
```

Properties are declared within the class in almost the same way as the variables discussed earlier. The only difference is that the properties have an access modifier of *private*, which limits the access to the property to the class itself. PHP actually does not enforce this and does allow you to directly change the values in a property. However, this weakens the power of classes to verify that data passed into the class is valid before it is saved.

Properties set to *private* must be indirectly accessed and modified by *get* and *set methods*. Get methods return the value contained in a property to the program which made an instance (object) of the class itself.

```php
<?php
    class Lion {
        private $color = "no color";
        private $weight = 0;
        function get_color() {
            return $this->color;
        }
        function get_weight() {
            return $this->weight;
        }
    }
?>
```

In this example, the get_color method returns the contents of the $color property. The get_weight method returns the contents of the $weight property.

Set methods provide the user of the class (object) the ability to change the contents within the properties.

```php
<?php
    class Lion {
            private $color = "no color";
            private $weight = 0;
            function get_color() {
                    return $this->color;
            }
            function get_weight() {
                    return $this->weight;
            }
            function set_color($value) {
                    $this->color = $value;
            }
            function set_weight($value) {
                    if ($value > 0) {
                            $this->weight = $value;
                    }
            }
    }

?>
```

Set methods can (and should) verify the data passed. In the preceding example, the weight is verified to be more than zero before the new weight is saved. If the weight passed is not valid, the update is ignored. The class could raise an exception for the calling program to handle when problems occur.

■ **Note**　$this-> is a pointer which tells the system to use the private property created in the top of the current object of the class.

```php
<?php
    require_once("lion.php");
    $fred = new Lion;
    print $fred->get_weight(); // 0
    print $fred->get_color(); // no color
    $fred->set_color("Yellow");
    print $fred->get_color(); // Yellow
    $fred->set_weight(50);
    print $fred->get_weight(); // 50
?>
```

Classes are usually contained in separate files (with the class name and .php) to allow them to be used in multiple programs. They can then be pulled into a calling program using one of the methods previously discussed. An instance of the class (an object) must be given a name ($fred in the preceding). This name is then used to point to the methods (or properties) to be used within the object. In the preceding example, the get methods are used to display the initial values of the properties. The set methods change these values and the get methods are called again to display the changes.

There is a lot more to learn about php syntax, along with class, properties, and methods. Hopefully, this quick introduction has provided a general understanding which might inspire you to study the topic more in-depth. Now that you have seen a quick review of the PHP language, let's take a more in-depth look at arrays.

EXERCISES

(You can download all working examples from this chapter at www.littleoceanwaves.com/arrays/)

1. Create a PHP program that contains an array with your name, address, and phone number. The program should display the contents of the array to the user.

2. When should conditional statements be used?

3. When is it a good idea to use a function?

4. Why is the foreach loop a good choice when working with arrays?

5. Using the php.net web site, explain the difference between the print and echo statements.

CHAPTER 2

Simple Arrays

After completing this chapter, the student will be able to...

>Define and describe the advantages in using arrays

>Create an html form that validates information containing an html array

>Create a simple PHP array

>Save values into a simple PHP array

>Display values in a simple array

>Add values from an html form into a simple array

>Validate values before placing them into an array

2.1   What Are Arrays? Why Do We Need to Use Them?

Whenever a program uses information, that information must be stored in the memory of the computer. Individual information can be stored by creating a property.

```
$propertyname = value;
```

Property names are declared using the $ and a descriptive name for the property. PHP property names begin with a lowercase letter. If the programmer wants to use more than one word for the name, the camel case format and/or separation of the words via a special character (usually the _) can be used.

```
$firstName = "";
$first_Name = "";
$first_name = "";
```

Property names should be meaningful to make your program more readable.

```
$a = "";
$last_name = "";
```

In this example, *$a* is not meaningful. We do not have any indication of what might be stored. However, *$last_name* is meaningful; we understand that a person's last name will be stored. PHP itself will not stop you from declaring a property with a capital letter. However, that is usually reserved for class names and constants.

© Steve Prettyman 2017
S. Prettyman, *PHP Arrays*, DOI 10.1007/978-1-4842-2556-1_2

Let's take a quick look at a coding example that stores information using a property (or variable). Our example program will request personal information (such as name, address, city, state, ZIP) from a user via a web form (see Figure 2-1).

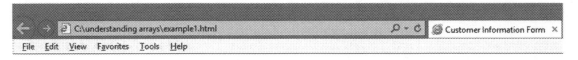

Please enter information in all fields

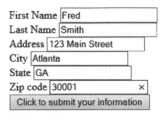

Figure 2-1. *example1.html*

Example 2-1. example1.html

```
<!DOCTYPE html>
<html lan='en'>
<head>
<title>Customer Information Form</title>
</head>
<body>
<form method='post' action='process_customer.php'>
<h2>Please enter information in all fields</h2>
First Name <input type='text' pattern='[a-zA-Z ]*' title='15 or less alphabetic characters'
maxlength='15' name='first_name' id='first_name' /><br />
Last Name <input type='text' pattern='[a-zA-Z ]*' title='20 or less alphabetic characters'
maxlength='20' name='last_name' id='last_name' /><br />
Address <input type='text' title='30 or less characters' maxlength='30' name='address'
id='address' /><br />
City <input type='text' pattern='[a-zA-Z ]*'  title='20 or less characters' maxlength='20'
name='city' id='city' /><br />
State <input type='text' pattern='[a-zA-Z ]*'  title='2 characters' maxlength='2'
name='state' id='state' /><br />
Zip code <input type='number' min='11111' max='99999' title='5 numerical characters'
name='zip_code' id='zip_code' /><br />
<input type='submit' value="Click to submit your information" />
</form>
</body>
</html>
```

Example 2-1 provides a pretty typical web form that requests information from the user. The html shown also filters the information accepted by the user, using html 5, to ensure that information was provided in the proper format.

▓ **Note** If you don't know html, you should review some of the free tutorials and videos provided on the web. PHP is a web application language which commonly interfaces with html and JavaScript.

Once the user enters the information in the proper format and hits the submit button, the information will be sent to a program on the web server for processing.

```
<form method='post' action='process_customer.php'>
```

In this example, the html form line indicates that the *process_customer.php* application will accept and handle the information.

When the information is sent, it is actually sent as a series of properties and values (also called keys and values). The property names are determined from the values shown in the *name* attributes of the html form (such as *first_name* in the preceding example). The *values* assigned to the properties are retrieved from the information entered by the user in the textboxes.

Example 2-2. Properties and values sent to process_customer.php

```
first_name = "Fred"
last_name = "Smith"
address = "123 Main Street"
city = "Atlanta"
state = "GA"
zip_code = "30001"
```

The properties created by html are very similar to properties used in PHP. This allows them to be easily processed within a PHP program. Both PHP and html create properties when they are first used. PHP considers the data type of any information that is displayed or received from an html web site to be *string*. Thus, as shown in Example 2-2, even though the html form requires the user to enter a number for the ZIP code, the value is actually stored as a string (indicated by the quotes).

PHP dynamically determines a property's data type when a value is stored into the property. This can have advantages and disadvantages. One advantage is the ability for PHP to change the data type of information stored in a property at any time.

```
$zip_code = "30001";
$zip_code = 30001;
```

The first statement in the preceding would place the string "*30001*" into the property *$zip_code*. If the property did not exist before, it would also be created. The second statement would change the type of information stored in *$zip_code* from a string to an integer.

Example 2-3. process_customer.php

```
<?php
// accepts information from example1.html
// This is NOT a complete program.
//The validate methods shown need to be created to clean any input.
$first_name = validate_first_name($_POST['first_name']);
```

```
$last_name = validate_last_name($_POST['last_name']);
$address = validate_address($_POST['address']);
$city = validate_city($_POST['city']);
$state = validate_state($_POST['state']);
$zip_code = validate_zip_code($_POST['zip_code']);
print "Your name is $first_name $last_name.";
print "You live at $address, $city, $state, $zip_code";
?>
```

A PHP program can access information passed from an html form using the *$_POST* or *$_GET* methods. The method used in the PHP program must match the *type* indicated in the html *form* attribute. Information passed via *post* will not display in the *URL* address in the browser. Information passed via *get* will display on the *URL* line.

2.1.1 Why Do We Have a Choice?

Information passed via *get* does not use as much server memory because it is contained in the URL address. Information passed via *post* resides in the memory of the server. Sites that have heavy traffic, such as search engines, use *get* to be as memory efficient as possible. Although passing information via *post* 'hides' the information from the URL line, it is not considered to be secure because it is not usually encrypted.

The *$_POST* and *$_GET* methods use the property name created by the html form (*'first_name'*) to retrieve the value passed (*'Fred'*). The information can then be placed into a property (*$first_name*) that is defined in the program itself. Remember, all the information gathered via the *$_POST* (or *$_GET*) method is stored as the *string* data type (since the html form can only pass strings).

Since PHP dynamically creates a property the first time it is used, space is allocated in memory for the property and its value by the operating system of the web server.

```
$first_name = validate_first_name($_POST['first_name']);
```

This line will pull the data from the *first_name* html textbox which resides in the form. It will validate the data, and if the data is valid, it will create the property *$first_name* and place the information into the property (in memory). The same process occurs for the other lines in the preceding example, except for the *print* statement. The *print* statement will display each of the values currently in the properties.

■ **Note** It is very important to validate any information received from a client machine before placing it into properties in a program. This example indicates that several validate methods (such as 'validate_first_name') exist in the program to accomplish this task.

```
declare(strict_types=1);
function validate_first_name(string $value) : string
        {
                If ((strlen($value) <= 0) || (strlen($value) > 15))
                {
                        throw new Exception("Invalid First Name");
                }
                return $value;
        }
```

```php
function validate_last_name(string $value) : string
{
        If ((strlen($value) <= 0) || (strlen($value) > 20))
        {
                throw new Exception("Invalid Last Name");
        }
        return $value;
}
function validate_address(string $value) : string
{
        If ((strlen($value) <= 0) || (strlen($value) > 30))
        {
                throw new Exception("Invalid Address");
        }
                return $value;
        }

function validate_city(string $value) : string
{
        If ((strlen($value) <= 0) || (strlen($value) > 20))
        {
                throw new Exception("Invalid City");
        }
        return $value;
}
function validate_state(string $value) : string
{
        If ((strlen($value) <= 0) || (strlen($value) > 2))
        {
                throw new Exception("Invalid State");
        }
        return $value;
}
function validate_zip_code(string $value) : string
{
        If ((strlen($value) <= "11111") || (strlen($value) > "99999"))
        {
                throw new Exception("Invalid Zip Code");
        }
        return $value;
}
?>
```

The validation methods shown in this example validate the values for the same type of information as was shown on the html form. For example *first_name* is alphabetic, with 15 or fewer characters. If the data is not valid, a *user exception* can be thrown and then caught by the calling program to inform the user of any problems.

Remember that the values have already been validated in the html form. If the data is not valid when it arrives in the PHP program, then the data was corrupted. It is logical and appropriate that an exception should be raised when this occurs.

31

The *validate_first_name* function shown uses *strnlen* to determine if the string passed from the html form meets these requirements. If it does, the value is returned so it can be placed into the *$first_name* property. If the information is not valid an exception is thrown with the message *"Invalid First Name."*

Once these statements execute, the customer information is stored in memory and can be accessed by the program. If this was a complete program, the information would also be stored in a location external to the program (such as a database or cloud location) before the program completes execution. Once the program execution ends, the data is no longer accessible in memory. When a program completes, the garbage collector of the operating system is notified that the memory space is no longer needed. The garbage collector then takes the responsibility to reassign the memory space for other uses.

This process becomes more complicated, however, if the program needs the ability to store information from multiple customers.

```
$c1_first_name = ...
$c1_last_name = ...
$c1_address = ...
$c1_city = ...
$c1_state = ...
$c1_zip_code = ...
$c2_first_name = ...
$c2_last_name = ...
$c2_address = ...
$c2_city = ...
$c2_state = ...
$c2_zip_code = ...
```

The programmer could choose to create properties for every customer, in a format similar to the preceding. However, there are several problems with this approach. First, the programmer might end up having to create a lot of properties to handle a lot of customers. If in this example we expect just 100 customers, we would need 600 properties to hold all the information! This does not seem very reasonable or very efficient. Second, in most cases the programmer and the company do not know exactly how many customers will exist. It is probably not possible to determine an exact number. This is where arrays come in handy.

An *array* is nothing more than a container of multiple properties. The array is given a name (such as *$customer_records*) using the same syntax as a property. This one name is then used for storing and reviewing every value in the array. Since the same name is used to access every value in the array, there needs to be a way to determine where a value is being stored or retrieved. This is done by using a *subscript*. In most languages a subscript is a numerical value. However, as we will see later, PHP arrays also allow alphabetic subscripts.

▨ **Note** PHP actually has only one type of arrays. This type allows numerical or alphabetic subscripts. The term "Associative Arrays" is used to describe PHP arrays with alphabetic subscripts. However, all PHP arrays are stored in memory in the same format. We will discuss associative arrays a little later.

We can replace the individual properties (such as *$first_name*) with the array name plus a subscript (*$customer_records[0]*).

Example 2-4. process_customer_record.php

```php
<?php
// accepts information from example1.html
// This is NOT a complete program.
//The validate methods shown need to be created to clean any input
$customer_record[0] = validate_first_name($_POST['first_name']);
$customer_record[1] = validate_last_name($_POST['last_name']);
$customer_record[2] = validate_address($_POST['address']);
$customer_record[3] = validate_city($_POST['city']);
$customer_record[4] = validate_state($_POST['state']);
$customer_record[5] = validate_zip_code($_POST['zip_code']);
print "Your name is $customer_record[0] $customer_record[1].";
print "You live at $customer_record[2], $customer_record[3]";
print " $customer_record[4], $customer_record[5]";
?>
```

In Example 2-4, the individual records are replaced with locations within the array *$customer_record* to store the values retrieved. In most programming languages, array subscripts must be numbered beginning with zero. Unlike many other languages, PHP allows us to dynamically create our array locations when needed (as shown in Example 2-4). This allows us store and revive values in an array in a similar way to storing and retrieving values in properties.

In PHP, we do not have to include the subscript when storing values into an array.

Example 2-5. process_customer_record.php

```php
// accepts information from example1.html
// This is NOT a complete program. The validate  methods shown //need to be created to clean
any iinput
$customer_record[] = validate_first_name($_POST['first_name']);
$customer_record[] = validate_last_name($_POST['last_name']);
$customer_record[] = validate_address($_POST['address']);
$customer_record[] = validate_city($_POST['city']);
$customer_record[] = validate_state($_POST['state']);
$customer_record[] = validate_zip_code($_POST['zip_code']);
print "Your name is $customer_record[0] $customer_record[1].";
print "You live at $customer_record[2], $customer_record[3],";
print "$customer_record[4], $customer_record[5].";
?>
```

We do, however, still need to understand that the array subscripts will be automatically assigned a number (beginning with 0) as each value is placed in the array. Example 2-4 and Example 2-5 actually produce the same array. Notice, in Example 2-5, to retrieve the individual values in the array, we still have to be aware of the subscript. We can use a *foreach* loop to pull all values without knowing the subscript (as we will see shortly). We can also use the PHP function *print_r* as seen in the following to quickly view all contents of an array.

PHP arrays have several advantages over arrays in other languages.

```php
$customer_record[0] =
        validate_first_name($_POST['first_name']);
$customer_record[2] =
        validate_last_name($_POST['last_name']);
```

If a position in an array is not given an initial value in a language like Java, that position would hold a *null* value. A null value is not zero, and it is not empty. If the Java program attempts to perform a calculation on a value in the array that has not been given a value, the program would produce an error indicating that a null value was in that position. **If a position is skipped in a PHP array, that position merely does not exist.**

```
print_r($customer_record);
Array ( [0] => Fred [2] => Smith [3] => 123 Main Street [4] => Atlanta [5] => GA [6] =>
30001 )
```

As you can see from the results of executing a *print_r* statement against a populated *$customer_record* array, there is no position 1 that exists in the array.

```
You might wonder if this will cause any problems in retrieving values from the array.
```

Remember that when creating dynamic arrays in PHP we might not know how many positions are in the array. You may have seen or been taught to use the *for loop* with arrays. **The for loop is not the best choice for retrieving values in a PHP array.**

The *foreach loop* is a much better choice. This loop will automatically only retrieve positions that exist in the array (it would skip position 1 in the preceding example) and automatically retrieve all positions of an array.

```
foreach( $customer_record as $value)
{
        print $value;
}
```

$customer_record is the name of the array. *as* is a required keyword. *$value* represents the value that exists within the position that the method is currently accessing. *$value* can be assigned any name by the programmer. It is a temporary property that holds the value in the current position in the array.

If we use this loop to print the values in the previous array, the loop would start at position 0 and print the contents of the first position (*Fred*). The loop would then move to the next position in the array, position 2 (there is no position 1). It would print the contents of this position (*Smith*) and continue until all positions in the array have been printed.

```
Fred Smith 123 Main Street Atlanta GA 30001
```

The *foreach loop* makes retrieving values from PHP arrays easy. Using this loop will eliminate any possibility of trying to retrieve values from nonexistent positions in the array and also the possibility of going beyond the end (size of) the array. The size and positions of an array could change at any time, and this little *foreach loop* will still function properly. We will also discover that there are many PHP functions that eliminate the need to use loops when reading, retrieving, or updating values in an array.

2.2   Other Ways to Define Arrays

In PHP, if you know the initial values for an array, it can be created using a structure similar to other languages.

```
$customer_record = array('Fred', 'Smith', '123 Main Street', 'Atlanta', 'GA', '30001');
print_r($customer_record);
Array ( [0] => Fred [1] => Smith [2] => 123 Main Street [3] => Atlanta [4] => GA [5] =>
30001 )
```

In this example, we have initially created the array with a certain number of elements (six) and initial values. PHP, like other languages, will automatically number the subscripts for each position, beginning at zero. Since PHP stores all arrays in the same format, we can change the values in this array using the same techniques we have discussed.

```
$customer_record[0] = 'Pete';
print_r($customer_record);
Array ( [0] => Pete [1] => Smith [2] => 123 Main Street [3] => Atlanta [4] => GA [5] => 30001 )
```

As you can see, *Fred* is replaced by *Pete* by passing a new value into the proper position.

What happens if we attempt to place a value in a position that does not exist?

```
$customer_record[6] = '7707777777';
print_r($customer_record);
Array ( [0] => Pete [1] => Smith [2] => 123 Main Street [3] => Atlanta [4] => GA [5] =>
30001 [6] => 7707777777 )
```

As you can see, the array simply creates a new position and places the value in that position.

```
$customer_record[] = '7707777777';
```

PHP arrays will automatically place new values at the end of the array if a position is not included. This is not true in other languages. Many languages will indicate that you are out of bounds (you have exceeded the size of the array). They will not let you add elements to the array unless you somehow increase the size of the array.

In the format used in the preceding example, the original array contains the exact same information and positions as the previous array. PHP allows us to easily *append* a value to the end of any existing array, no matter how it was declared initially.

What happens if we load a number into a position in this array instead of a string?

```
$customer_record[5] = 30001;
Array ( [0] => Pete [1] => Smith [2] => 123 Main Street [3] => Atlanta [4] => GA [5] => 30001 )
```

The output of a *print_r* statement would produce similar results (because it makes no indication of the data types of the individual values).

However, we can detect the difference if we first convert our array to *JSON* format (using the method *json_encode*) and then display the results. We could also use the PHP *var_dump* method. We will look at examples using this method in a later chapter.

```
$json = json_encode($customer_record);
print_r($json);
["Pete","Smith","123 Main Street","Atlanta","GA",30001]
```

The JSON format allows you to see that the data type for the ZIP code did actually change from a string value ('30001') to a numeric value (30001). Even if the ZIP code already existed in string format, when we replace it with a numerical value, that number (not string) would now exist in the array.

2.3   Html Arrays

Now that we have a general idea of how arrays work in PHP, we can also use this concept with our html form and discover that we can easily pass an array into our PHP program.

Example 2-6. example1_array.html

```
<!DOCTYPE html>
<html lan='en'>
<head>
<title>Customer Information Form</title>
</head>
<body>
<form method='post' action=
'process_customer_array.php'>
<h2> Please enter information in all fields</h2>
First Name <input type='text' pattern='[a-zA-Z ]*' title='15 or less alphabetic characters'
maxlength='15' name='customer_record[0]' id='customer_record[0]' /><br />
Last Name <input type='text' pattern='[a-zA-Z ]*' title='20 or less alphabetic characters'
maxlength='20' name='customer_record[1]' id='customer_record[1]' /><br />
Address <input type='text' title='30 or less characters' maxlength='30' name='customer_
record[2]' id='customer_record[2]' /><br />
City <input type='text' pattern='[a-zA-Z ]*'  title='20 or less characters' maxlength='20'
name='customer_record[3]' id='customer_record[3]' /><br />
State <input type='text' pattern='[a-zA-Z ]*'  title='2 characters' maxlength='2'
name='customer_record[4]' id='customer_record[4]' /><br />
Zip code <input type='number' min='11111' max='99999' title='5 numerical characters'
name='customer_record[5]' id='customer_record[5]' /><br />
<input type='submit' value="Click to submit your information" />
</form>
</body>
</html>
```

In Example 2-5, each html *name* element has been replaced by a position in the *customer_record* array. This html array is dynamically created, just like PHP arrays. The value in the first textbox (which will be the customer's first name) is now placed into *customer_record[0]*.

The html form can now pass this array to the PHP program via the *post* method without any other changes.

Example 2-7. process_customer_array.php

```
<?php
$customer = filter_input_array(INPUT_POST);
$customer_record = validate_array($customer["customer_record"]);
print "Your name is $customer_record[0] $customer_record[1]. ";
print "You live at $customer_record[2], $customer_record[3],";
print "$customer_record[4], $customer_record[5]";
?>
```

As you can see from Example 2-7, we actually can use less coding to pull the html array into the program. The program includes a PHP *filter_input_array* method which pulls in the complete array created by the html form. It also filters out any harmful data (such as html symbols <>).

> ▓ **Note** The filter_input_array method would not verify that the fields have the correct information, such as 15 or fewer alphabetic characters in the first_name field (now called customer_record[0]). A validate_array method can be created to accept the array and pass individual values to the correct validation method.

```
function validate_array( $input_array)
{
$value = validate_first_name($input_array[0]);
$value = validate_last_name($input_array[1]);
$value = validate_address($input_array[2]);
$value = validate_city($input_array[3]);
$value = validate_state($input_array[4]);
$value = validate_zip_code($input_array[5]);
return $input_array;
}
```

Assuming that each of the validate methods will throw an exception if there is a problem, this method can assume every field is validated if the flow reaches the end of the method. The method returns the array passed so the array can be placed in *$customer_record*. $value does hold the individual values returned. However, it exists only to allow the individual validate methods to still include a return statement as shown previously. We could, of course remove the return statement and *$value* = would not be needed.

In Example 2-7, *$customer_record = validate_array($customer["customer_record"])* searches for the array named *customer_record* and places that array into *$customer_record* in the PHP program after calling *validate_array*. This actually turns $customer_record into an array of the values passed from the textboxes on the form. There is no longer a need to populate individual positions in *$customer_record* via additional PHP code. This was all completed with one code line!

2.3.1   Deleting

```
Array (
[0] => Fred [1] => Smith [2] => 123 Main Street [3] => Atlanta [4] => GA [5] => 30001
)
```

A programming logic textbook would explain the necessity to create a loop to remove a value in the middle of an array like the preceding. If we were to remove the second value ([1]), the textbook would explain that each value after the one removed (*'123 Main Street,' 'Atlanta,' 'GA,' 30001*) would need to be repositioned into the subscript above it to fill in the value that was removed. This is usually necessary to avoid any *NULL* values.

```
Array (
[0] => Fred [1] => 123 Main Street [2] => Atlanta [3] => GA [4] => 30001
)
```

The loop would update the array to something similar to the preceding example.

In PHP, this is not necessary. As explained earlier, PHP arrays work very well with missing subscripts. The *foreach* loop automatically skips over missing subscripts. Thus, we can remove any subscript from an array by creating a very simple function.

Example 2-8. deletesubscript.php

```
declare(strict_types=1);
function delete_array_value(int $subscript)
{

        $customer_record =
        array('Pete' ,'Smith' ,'123 Main Street' ,'Atlanta','GA', 30001);
        unset($customer_record[$subscript]);
}
delete_array_value(1);
```

Example 2-8 uses the method *unset* to remove whatever subscript is passed into the function *delete_array_value*. In this example the delete method would remove the location of *Smith* from the array. The array would now contain

```
$customer_record =
        array('Pete','123 Main Street' ,'Atlanta','GA', 30001);
```

If we execute the following statement, you will see that the subscript and its value have been removed.

```
Print_r($customer_record);
Array (
        [0] => Pete
        [2] => 123 Main Street
        [3] => Atlanta
        [4] => GA
        [5] => 30001
}
```

2.4   Updating & Inserting

Actually, we have already shown several examples on updating values in arrays. Let's look at another.

Example 2-9. insert.php

```
function insert_array_value( $value )
{

        $customer_record =
        array('Pete' ,'Smith' ,'123 Main Street' ,'Atlanta','GA', 30001);
        array_push($customer_record, $value);
}
insert_array_value('770-777-7777');
```

In Example 2-9, the function *array_push* is used to add values to the end of the array. The phone number would be placed into position 6 in the *$customer_record* array just after the ZIP code.

To create an update method, we can just make a slight change to this example.

Example 2-10. update.php

```
declare(strict_types=1);

function update_array_value( int $position, $value )
{

        $customer_record =
        array('Pete' ,'Smith' ,'123 Main Street' ,'Atlanta','GA', 30001);
        $customer_record[$position] = $value;
}
update_array_value(0, 'Peter');
```

In Example 2-10, both the position (subscript) and the value are passed into the function. The array is then updated by passing the value into the location in the *$customer_record* array.

Let's look at a method that combines these ideas.

Example 2-11. update_insert_value.php

```
declare(strict_types=1);

function update_array_value( $value, int $subscript = -1)
{

        $customer_record =
        array('Pete' ,'Smith' ,'123 Main Street' ,'Atlanta','GA', 30001);

        If( $subscript != -1)
        {
                $customer_record[$subscript] = $value;
        }
        else
        {
                array_push($customer_record, $value);
        }
}
update_array_value("770-777-7777", 6);
update_array_value("770-777-7777");
update_array_value("Peter", 0);
```

This update method allows us to insert individual values or actually replace values. If the subscript is passed, then the value passed is placed into the location requested. If a subscript is not provided, the *array_push* function is called to place the value at the end of the array.

```
update_array_value("770-777-7777", 6);
```

Using this statement, the phone number would be placed in position six. Even though there is not a position six in this example, PHP will create a position six, as we have seen from other examples. Thus, this call is actually inserting the phone number.

```
update_array_value("770-777-7777");
```

Using this format causes the *$subscript* to be set to –1 since a default value was provided in the function declaration statement.

```
function update_array_value( $value, int $subscript = -1)
```

This will cause the else part of the if statement to execute.

```
If( $subscript != -1)
```

The *array_push* function will then be used to insert the phone number at the end of the array. This also places the phone number in position six.

```
update_array_value("Peter", 0);
```

This final statement passes both an existing subscript and a value. This would cause the top of the if statement to execute. The value (*Peter*) would replace the current value in position 0.

As you will see frequently, once you get used to using arrays, you will find the amount of code needed to process the information is much less. Example 2-7 has only four executable statements. Example 2-3 (and Example 2-4) had seven executable statements. **This demonstrates that using arrays is more efficient than using individual properties.** Arrays provide us the ability to expand (or contact) their size, and allow us to easily adjust the data types stored.

Before we look at multidimensional arrays, let's take a break and do some practice exercises.

EXERCISES

(You can download all working examples from this chapter at www.littleoceanwaves.com/arrays/)

1. Create an html form to accept information about a book (such as book name, book author, publisher, ISBN number). Use html 5 to validate the input provided by the user. Pass the information into a PHP program, which will then display the information back to the user.

2. How does using arrays make a program more efficient?

3. How are PHP arrays different from arrays in other programming languages?

CHAPTER 3

■ ■ ■

Multidimensional Arrays

After completing this chapter, the student will be able to...

Define and describe the advantages in using multidimensional arrays

Compare a table with a multidimensional array

Create a multidimensional PHP array

Save values into a multidimensional PHP array

Display values in a multidimensional array

Add values from an html form into a multidimensional array

Validate values before placing them into a multidimensional array

Convert JSON data read from a text file into a PHP array

Convert PHP arrays to JSON objects and save to a text file

Save array information to a MySQL Database

The previous chapter showed us how efficient arrays can be.
However, the question that was not answered is

"How do we handle data from multiple customers?"

A simple array holds information that is related to a particular individual component, such as a customer. In order to hold all of a customer's information in memory, we must think in more than one *dimension*. We need to have the ability to hold multiple components of customer information. We can think of a doctor's office (before everything became computerized) keeping records of each patient in a file, with all the files for all the patients being stored within a file cabinet.

Multidimensional arrays work in a similar way. A customer's information is stored in a *'record'* (similar to the file in the doctor's office). In our previous example, all of the information related to *Fred Smith* is kept together in a *'record'*. Multiple records (just like the file cabinet) are kept together in a *'table'*. The *'table'* would contain all of the customer records.

Spreadsheets work in the same way.

In Table 3-1, four customers exist within the table. In a spreadsheet or in a program, the information for each customer is contained in a *record* (also referred to as a *row*). Each *row* has the same type of information in each *column*. For example, the first *column* contains the first name of each of the customers.

© Steve Prettyman 2017
S. Prettyman, *PHP Arrays*, DOI 10.1007/978-1-4842-2556-1_3

Table 3-1. *Customers Table*

First Name	Last Name	Address	City	State	Zip Code
"Pete"	"Smith"	"123 Main Street"	"Atlanta"	"GA"	30001
"Sally"	"Parisi"	"101 South Street"	"Atlanta"	"GA"	30001
"Jake"	"Boukari"	"111 Peachtree Street"	"Atlanta"	"GA"	30011
"Cap"	"Hill"	"1112 Ptree-Dunwoody Rd"	"Atlanta"	"GA"	30018

This table contains six columns and four rows. However, remember that spreadsheets and programs begin the numbering of elements with zero, not one. The uppermost left element (which contains *"Pete"*) resides in row zero and column zero (0, 0). The lowermost right element (*30018*) resides in row three and column 5 (3, 5).

> *What resides in row 2 and column 2? "111 Peachtree Street"*

> *Why do we say row x and column y, not column y and row x?*

The answer lies in how the information is stored in memory. The operating system stores two-dimensional arrays by row. The rows are kept intact because everything in a row is related (all of *Pete Smith's* information). The row information is placed in memory locations that are contiguous to each other (next to each other). Other rows are not necessarily stored in memory next to previous rows. This allows the operating system to be efficient with memory storage.

When retrieving data from a *two-dimensional array*, we usually retrieve or look at a row of information at a time (such as all of *Pete Smith's* information). This in turn allows the operating system to go to one continuous area of memory to pull the information. When a column of information is needed, less efficiently occurs, because the operating system might need to go to several noncontiguous locations in memory to retrieve the information.

When we store information into a table, or array, we also (usually) store a complete row of information first (all of *Pete Smith's* information) before storing another row of information. This again maps to the operating system storing all the related information into the same general location of memory before it saves the next row of information (possibly at a completely different location in memory).

All this just reminds us **to always list the row first and then the column when saving or retrieving information in a *two-dimensional* array.**

```
print $customer_record[0];
```

In Chapter 1, we discovered that the preceding statement would print out the first name of the customer (*'Pete'*). However, if the array is *two-dimensional*, this statement will pull the complete first row, instead of the first record. To read a specific record, both the row and column must be specified.

```
print $customer_record[1][0];
```

In this statement, the first subscript indicates row (1), and the second subscript indicates column (0). If Table 3-1 is an array, this statement would print *Sally*.

> *What would print $customer_record[2][4]; display? GA*

To dynamically create a two-dimensional array in PHP, we use almost the same statements that we used for a single dimension.

```
$customer_record[0][0] = "Pete";
$customer_record[0][1] = "Smith";
$customer_record[0][2] = "123 Main Street";
$customer_record[0][3] = "Atlanta";
$customer_record[0][4] = "GA";
$customer_record[0][5] = 30001;
$customer_record[1][0] = "Sally";
$customer_record[1][1] = "Parisi";
$customer_record[1][2] = "101 South Street";
$customer_record[1][3] = "Atlanta";
$customer_record[1][4] = "GA";
$customer_record[1][5] = 30001;
```

Let's look at what we see when we use the *print_r* method on the array we just created.

```
print_r($customer_record);
Array (
[0] =>
        Array ([0] => Pete
                [1] => Smith
                [2] => 123 Main Street
                [3] => Atlanta
                [4] => GA
                [5] =>30001 )
[1] =>
        Array ([0] => Sally
                [1] => Parisi
                [2] => 101 South Street
                [3] => Atlanta
                [4] => GA
                [5] => 30001 )
)
```

■ **Note** The print_r method will display the preceding information without the line breaks that have been added.

The outside array (*Array ( )*) controls the rows, which are actually their own arrays. In this example, there are two rows indicated by [0]=> and [1]=> (on the lines by themselves). Inside of each row is an *Array* that controls the columns for that row. The first *Array* contains the information about *Pete Smith*. The second *Array* contains information about *Sally Parisi*. You should notice that these arrays are exactly the same format as the one-dimensional array that we discussed in Chapter 1. **In PHP, two-dimensional arrays are actually individual one-dimensional arrays held together by an array that surrounds them.**

Can we create this two-dimensional array without specifying the subscript numbers (as shown with one-dimensional arrays)?

When using the dynamic approach of creating the positions when needed, we have to tell PHP when to start a new array or row (when to switch from the array which contains the *Pete* information to the array that contains the *Sally* information). One way we can do this is by using a *counting variable*.

Example 3-1. process_customer_twodim.php

```php
<?php
$I = -1;
$customer_record[++$I][] = 'Pete';
$customer_record[$I][] = 'Smith';
$customer_record[$I][] = '123 Main Street';
$customer_record[$I][] = 'Atlanta';
$customer_record[$I][] = 'GA';
$customer_record[$I][] = 30001;
$customer_record[++$I][] = 'Sally';
$customer_record[$I][] = 'Parisi';
$customer_record[$I][] = '101 South Street';
$customer_record[$I][] = 'Atlanta';
$customer_record[$I][] = 'GA';
$customer_record[$I][] = 30001;
print_r($customer_record);
?>
```

In Example 3-1, A *counting variable $I* is created with an initial value of *–1*. In the next statement, the variable is incremented before it is used (*++$I*). The value in the variable (0) is used to define the initial subscript for the array containing the information for *Pete*. The remaining values for *Pete* are placed into the related array using *$I,* which is still set to 0 each time. When it is time to create the array holding the information for *Sally,* the *counting variable* is again incremented. This provides a subscript number of *1* for each value placed in the *Sally* array. Notice that we did not need to provide a value for any of the positions with the *Pete* or *Sally* array.

However, this is not the most efficient way! This is not good coding. Don't create your two-dimensional arrays using this example!

What would happen if we didn't place the counting variable or a number in the first subscript positions (such as $customer_record[][] = 'Pete';)?

Each value for *Pete* and *Sally* would end up with its own array and only one subscript. Each of the two subscripts would increment each time. Download Example 3-1 and remove every place that $I occurs and run the program to see the mess it would produce!

We could eliminate the need for using the counting variable if we define the complete array at one time.

```php
$customer_record = array (
        array('Pete' , 'Smith' , '123 Main Street' ,'Atlanta', 'GA', 30001),
        array('Sally' , 'Parisi' , '101 South Street' ,'Atlanta' , 'GA' , 30001)
);
```

This approach is a lot more efficient, taking a lot less code to create. It produces the same results as Example 3-1. You do need to be careful to include all the required commas as shown in the preceding. Also note that the semicolon is still needed at the end of the complete statement.

We can still change and add additional values in the array using the approach we have seen before.

```php
$customer_record[0][0] = 'Peter';
$customer_record[0][6] ='770-770-7777';
$customer_record[2] =
        array('Jake' , 'Boukari' ,'111 Peachtree Street' , 'Atlanta' ,'GA' , 30011);
```

```
Array (
        [0] =>
                Array ( [0] => Pete [1] => Peter [2] => 123 Main Street [3] => Atlanta
                        [4] => GA [5] => 30001 [6] => 770-770-7777 )
```

```
    [1] =>
            Array ( [0] => Sally [1] => Parisi [2] => 101 South Street [3] => Atlanta
                    [4] => GA [5] => 30001 )

    [2] =>  Array ( [0] => Jake [1] => Boukari [2] => 111 Peachtree Street [3] => Atlanta
                    [4] => GA [5] => 30011 )
)
```

PHP arrays allow a lot of flexibility. We are able to change a value in the original array (replacing *Pete* with *Peter*). We are able to add another value to the array containing *Peter* information (the array now contains his phone number). We were also able to add a completely new array inside the *customer_record* array (There is now a *Jake* array). To accomplish some of these tasks in other programming languages would take a lot more code.

However, we are not dynamically creating the array as we have seen previously. Soon we will see an example showing us how to dynamically create an array and add rows without knowing the size of the current array.

3.1   Html Arrays

This is all pretty neat, but can we still easily add customer information coming from a web page into our two-dimensional array as we did in Chapter 1?

The answer is YES!

Example 3-2. example2_array.html

```
<!DOCTYPE html>
<html lan='en'>
<head>
<title>Customer Information Form</title>
</head>
<body>
<form method='post' action='process_customer_array_twodim.php'>
<h2> Please enter information in all fields</h2>
First Name <input type='text' pattern='[a-zA-Z ]*' title='15 or less alphabetic characters'
maxlength='15' name='customer_record[0]' id='customer_record[0]' /><br />
Last Name <input type='text' pattern='[a-zA-Z ]*' title='20 or less alphabetic characters'
maxlength='20' name='customer_record[1]' id='customer_record[1]' /><br />
Address <input type='text' title='30 or less characters' maxlength='30' name='customer_
record[2]' id='customer_record[2]' /><br />
City <input type='text' pattern='[a-zA-Z ]*'  title='20 or less characters' maxlength='20'
name='customer_record[3]' id='customer_record[3]' /><br />
State <input type='text' pattern='[a-zA-Z ]*'  title='2 characters' maxlength='2'
name='customer_record[4]' id='customer_record[4]' /><br />
Zip code <input type='number' min='11111' max='99999' title='5 numerical characters'
name='customer_record[5]' id='customer_record[5]' /><br />
<input type='submit' value="Click to submit your information" />
</form>
</body>
</html>
```

The only change made to the html file (Example 3-2) is to change the name of the PHP program called (*process_customer_array_twodim.php*).

Example 3-3. process_customer_array_twodim.php

```php
<?php
$customer_record = array (
        array('Pete' , 'Smith' ,
                '123 Main Street' , 'Atlanta', 'GA', 30001),
        array('Sally' , 'Parisi' , '101 South Street' ,
                'Atlanta' , 'GA' , 30001)
);
$customer = filter_input_array(INPUT_POST);
$customer_info =validate_array($customer["customer_record"]);
array_push($customer_record, $customer_info);
print_r($customer_record);
?>
```

In Example 3-3, a two-dimensional array (*$customer_record*) is declared. The process to add the html data to the array requires only one additional line to be added to the example from Chapter 1. The PHP method *array_push* determines the size of an existing array and adds values to the end of an existing array. *$customer_info* contains the array of values the customer entered into the html form. *array_push* attaches this array to the end of the *$customer_record* array.

```
Array (
[0] =>
Array ( [0] => Pete [1] => Smith [2] => 123 Main Street [3] => Atlanta [4] => GA [5] =>
30001 )
[1] =>
Array ( [0] => Sally [1] => Parisi [2] => 101 South Street [3] => Atlanta [4] => GA [5] =>
30001 )
[2] =>
Array ( [0] => Fred [1] => Smith [2] => 123 Main Street [3] => Atlanta [4] => GA [5] =>
30001 ) )
```

All the values were appended to the end of the array with just one code statement!

▓ **Note**   We could also use array_push to add the Jake information shown in a previous example.

```
array_push($customer_record, array('Jake' , 'Boukari' , '111 Peachtree Street' , 'Atlanta' ,
'GA' , 30011));
```

This would eliminate the need to use a subscript (2 was used in the previous Jake example).

Let's take this example a step closer to the "real world." One shortcoming of this example is that the information is lost when the program ends. We can make a few changes to the code to read and save our array using a text file.

▓ **Note**   In the "real world," this information would probably be saved in a database. However, this example gives you a general idea of how easy it is to save information with PHP.

Example 3-4. process_customer_array_twodim_saved.php

```php
<?php
$customer_file = file_get_contents("customer_data.json");
$customer_record = json_decode($customer_file, TRUE);
$customer = filter_input_array(INPUT_POST);
$customer_info = validate_array($customer["customer_record"]);
array_push($customer_record, $customer_info);
print_r($customer_record);
file_put_contents("customer_data.json", json_encode($customer_record));
?>
```

A lot happens in Example 3-4. The PHP method *file_get_contents* will dump all the contents of a file into the property provided. The contents of the file *customer_data.json* are placed into the property *$customer_file* (which makes it an array).

```php
$customer_record = json_decode($customer_file, TRUE);
```

In this statement the contents of *$customer_file* are converted from JSON format to PHP array format using the PHP function *json_decode*. The file itself contains JSON data. The array created is placed into the property *$customer_record*. This automatically turns *$customer_record* into a two-dimensional array (assuming that the information in the file is formatted correctly).

```php
file_put_contents("customer_data.json", json_encode($customer_record));
```

After the html array is retrieved from the html form, added to the *$customer_record* array, and displayed, it is time to store the updated information. The PHP function *file_put_contents* will dump the contents of a property into a file. It will overwrite whatever is already in the file. It will also create the file if it does not exist.

However, remember it is assumed that JSON data is stored in the file. To convert the array into JSON format the PHP method *json_encode* is called. This converted JSON data is then stored in the file *customer_data.json*.

In just seven lines of code an array is populated from a file, data is retrieved from an html form and added to the array, and the data is then stored back into the file.

Let's make one last improvement to this program. If the data contained within the file is not a valid JSON format, PHP will produce an error message. Let's add some code to keep our program from crashing if the file is invalid or missing, or the data in the file not a valid JSON format.

Example 3-5. process_customer_array_twodim_saved_ex.php

```php
<?php
try
{
        $customer_file = file_get_contents("customer_data.json");
$customer_record = json_decode($customer_file, TRUE);
$customer =filter_input_array(INPUT_POST);
$customer_info =validate_array($customer["customer_record"]);
array_push($customer_record,$customer_info);
print_r($customer_record);
file_put_contents("customer_data.json", json_encode($customer_record));
}
```

```
catch(Exception $e)
{

        print "An Exception occurred. Message: " . $e->getMessage();
}
catch(Error $e)
{

        print "An Error occurred. Message: " . $e->getMessage();

}

?>
```

In PHP 7, the *try/catch* blocks are used to capture *Exceptions* and *Errors. Exceptions* are "user" exceptions that may be raised by the program. For example, a validation method (such as *validate_zip_code*) determines if the ZIP code information received from the html form is in the proper format. If the information is not valid, the method can *raise* an exception for the calling program to handle. If this occurred the flow of the code would jump to a *catch* block handling exception (if there is one).

In Example 3-5, *$e* holds the *Exception* object. The object includes a *getMessage* method which holds the actual error message produced. The *print* statement would display the error message. *User Exceptions* are not usually considered to be fatal. They should be handled by the program and execution of the program should continue, if possible.

Errors are produced by the PHP environment. An *error* could be produced if the file accessed does not exist. *Errors* can also be produced if there are syntax errors in the program code. In PHP 7, *Errors* can be handled in a similar fashion as *Exceptions.* In this example, any *error* is caught by the *catch* block for errors. The *Error* object also includes a *getMessage* method to display the error message. Unlike *Exceptions, Errors* are considered to be fatal. The program should be shut down when errors occur.

The use of both catch blocks in the example will ensure that we capture all possible problems with executing this program and display the messages related to the problems that might occur.

Now let's look at a quick MySQL database example.

Example 3-6. process_customer_array_twodim_saved_mysqli.php

```
try
{
$mysqli = new mysqli("localhostorwebsite", "userid", "password", "database");
$query = "SELECT * FROM customers";
$result = $mysqli->query($query);
$customer_record = $result->fetch_all(MYSQLI_NUM);
$customer = filter_input_array(INPUT_POST);
$customer_info = validate_array($customer["customer_record"]);
array_push($customer_record, $customer_info);
print_r($customer_record);
$query =
"INSERT INTO customers(first_name, last_name, address, city, state, zip_code) VALUES (";
$query .= $customer_info[0] . "," . $customer_info[1] . "," . $customer_info[2] . ",";
$query .= $customer_info[3] . "," . $customer_info[4] . "," . $customer_info[5] . ")";
$result = $mysqli->query($query);
$mysqli->close();
}
```

```
catch(Exception $e)
{

        print "An Exception occurred. Message: " . $e->getMessage();

}

catch(Error $e)
{

        print "An Error occurred. Message: " . $e->getMessage();

}
?>
```

Example 3-6 provides a very simplified example using a MySQL database.

```
$mysqli = new mysqli("localhostorwebsite", "userid", "password", "database");
```

The first line connects to MySQL and the database ("database") with the given userid and password. The first parameter should either include "localhost" or the URL address (or IP address) of the database location.

```
$query = "SELECT * FROM customers";
```

The second statement builds a SQL string to pull all the *customer* records from the database.

```
$result = $mysqli->query($query);
```

The third line executes the query and places the results in *$result.*

```
$customer_record = $result->fetch_all(MYSQLI_NUM);
```

The *fetch_all* method converts the database rows into a two-dimensional array (with numeric subscripts). The array is placed into *$customer_record.*
The next several lines are the same as the previous example.

```
$query =
"INSERT INTO customers(first_name, last_name, address, city, state, zip_code)
VALUES (";
$query .= $customer_info[0] . "," . $customer_info[1] . "," . $customer_info[2] . ",";
$query .= $customer_info[3] . "," . $customer_info[4] . "," . $customer_info[5] . ")";
```

After the information from the html form is attached to the *$customer_record* array (and displayed), a SQL INSERT string is created from the information gathered in the html form.

```
$result = $mysqli->query($query);
```

The *query* command then adds the record to the database.

```
$mysqli->close();
```

The close statement then closes the database connection. Any Exceptions or Errors are caught by the *catch* blocks.

There is no reason to reload all the records back into the database. In this example only the one record needs to be added to the current records.

Let's revisit the *foreach loop* to display information contained in two-dimensional arrays.

```
$customer_record = array (
        array('Pete' , 'Smith' , '123 Main Street' ,'Atlanta', 'GA', 30001),
        array('Sally' , 'Parisi' , '101 South Street' ,'Atlanta' , 'GA' , 30001)
);

foreach ($customer_record as $row)
{
        foreach($row as $column_value)
        {
                print $column_value . " ";
        }
}
```

```
foreach($customer_record as $row)
```

The first *foreach* statement contains the array name (*$customer_record*) and the row currently accessed by the loop (*$row*).

```
print_r($customer_record[]);
```

This is similar to only using one subscript when retrieving information from a two-dimensional array. The preceding statement will pull the current row (array) and display it. The outer *foreach* loop also pulls the current row (array) and places it in *$row*.

The first time the loop executes, it will be on row 0 (*Pete*). Each time flow of the program hits the bottom of the outer loop and then returns to the top, the *foreach* loop will move to the next row, until there are no more rows.

```
foreach($row as $column_value)
```

The internal loop moves through the value within each column for the row that has been selected by the outer *foreach* loop. *$row* contains all columns (values) in the current row. *$column_value* contains the contents of the current column. Each time the flow of the program hits the bottom of the inter loop and returns to the top of the inter *foreach* loop the next column is selected. When no more columns exist in the row, the loop ends.

When this occurs, the flow of the program will also drop to the bottom of the outside loop. This sends the flow back to the top of the outer loop, which retrieves the next row (if there is one).

```
print $column_value . " "
```

The print statement contained inside the inter loop displays the values in column within each row.

The format used in the preceding does not allow us to retrieve the actual row subscript number (0, 1) or the column subscript number (0, 1, 2, 3, 4, 5). To have access to this information we must break the *$row* property into two parts. Currently *$row* is the actual array (row) that will be accessed. To access the subscript we must request both the row subscript and the values in the row using the following format.

```
foreach( $customer_record as $row => $row_array )
{

        foreach( $row_array as $column => $column_value)
        {

                print "Row: $row Column: $column Value: $column_value ";

        }

        print "<br>";

}
```

```
Row: 0 Column: 0 Value: Pete Row: 0 Column: 1 Value: Smith Row: 0 Column: 2 Value: 123 Main
Street Row: 0 Column: 3 Value: Atlanta Row: 0 Column: 4 Value: GA Row: 0 Column: 5 Value:
30001
Row: 1 Column: 0 Value: Sally Row: 1 Column: 1 Value: Parisi Row: 1 Column: 2 Value: 101
South Street Row: 1 Column: 3 Value: Atlanta Row: 1 Column: 4 Value: GA Row: 1 Column: 5
Value: 30001
Row: 1 Column: 0 Value: Fred Row: 1 Column: 1 Value: Smith Row: 1 Column: 2 Value: 123 Main
Street Row: 1 Column: 3 Value: Atlanta Row: 1 Column: 4 Value: GA Row: 1 Column: 5 Value:
30001
```

This style is commonly referred to as the *$key => $value* format. The loop shown in the preceding uses *$row* instead of *$key* and *$row_array* instead of *$value*. It also uses *$column* instead of *$key* and *$column_value* instead of *$value*. The programmer can use any name for the key and value properties.

The format becomes clear when looking at the *print* statement and the output from the print statement. It is clear that *$row* now contains the actual row subscript, *$column* contains the column subscript, and *$column_value* contains the value in the row and column specified.

foreach loops can also be used to populate an array with values. It is common practice to provide initial values in an array, especially if the array will be used in calculations. In Chapter 1, we talked about the possibility that an array, in some program languages, could contain a *NULL* value. If an attempt is made to do a calculation on a position in an array that contains a *NULL* value, an *error* will be thrown. This can be avoided by providing initial values.

```
foreach( $customer_record as $row => $row_array)
{

        foreach( $row_array as $column => $column_value)
        {

                $customer_record[$row][$column] = "default";

        }
}
```

This code will place *"default"* in every position in the array. Remember, in many situations, the loading of initial values in a PHP array is not necessary because the array positions can be created and populated with actual values at the same time. Some programmers still choose to initialize values to be consistent with the logic used in other programming languages.

PHP also provides the method *array_fill* which will accomplish the same task as the previous example.

```
$customer_record =
      array_fill(0, 3, array_fill(0, 5, "default"));
```

The statement will create and fill each position in a *$customer_record* two-dimensional array with the value *"default."*

The *array_fill* syntax is as follows:

```
Array name =
      array_fill(first subscript in array,
            last subscript in array,
            value used to fill array);
```

In the example, four rows are created (0, 1, 2, 3) as indicated by 0, 3. Each row contains an array (as shown by the third position creating another array) with six columns (0, 1, 2, 3, 4, 5) as indicated by 0, 5. The limitation of using this method is that we need to know the initial size of the array. Of course, we can always add more rows and columns as needed.

```
$customer_record =
      array_fill(0, 5, "default");
```

For a one-dimensional array, we include the starting subscript (0), the ending subscript (5), and the value we want to place in each position (*"default"*).

The same logic shown in this chapter can be used for arrays that have more than two dimensions. The number of subscripts is determined by the number of dimensions, as is the number of *foreach* loops.

```
$square_array[$height][$length][$width] = 123;

foreach( $square_array as $height => $height_array)
{
      foreach( $height_array as $length => $length_array)
      {
            foreach( $length_array as $width => $width_value)
            {
$square_array[$height][$length][$width] = 123;

foreach( $square_array as $height => $height_array)
{
      foreach( $height_array as $length => $length_array)
      {
            foreach( $length_array as $width => $width_value)
            {
                  print $width_value;
                  $square_array[$height][$length][$width]= 345;
            }
      }
}
123
```

This loop will traverse through the three-dimensional array *$square_array* to display the value(s) in the array and then change the value(s) for each position to *345*.

3.2   Deleting

Example 3-7. deletesubscript.php

```
declare(strict_types=1);
function delete_array_value(int $subscript)
{

        $customer_record = array (
                        array('Pete' ,'Smith' ,'123 Main Street' ,'Atlanta','GA', 30001),
                        array('Sally' ,'Parisi' ,'101 South Street' ,'Atlanta' , 'GA' , 30001)
                        );
        unset($customer_record[$subscript]);

}

delete_array_value(1);
```

Example 3-7 previously demonstrated the removal of a subscript within a one-dimensional array. However, no changes (except for the array itself) are needed if the user wants to delete a row from a two-dimensional array. In this example the *Sally* array would be removed.

If we are using a two-dimensional array and want to remove one value from one of the rows, we can make a minor adjustment to our example.

Example 3-8. deletesubscript2dim.php

```
declare(strict_types=1);
function delete_array_value(int $first_subscript, int $second_subscript)
{

        $customer_record = array (
                array('Pete' ,'Smith' ,'123 Main Street' ,'Atlanta','GA', 30001),
                array('Sally' ,'Parisi' ,'101 South Street' ,'Atlanta' , 'GA' , 30001)
        )
unset($customer_record[$first_subscript][$second_subscript]);
}
delete_array_value(1,1);
```

In this example, after adding a second subscript, 'Parisi' would be removed.

3.2.1   Updating & Inserting

Actually we have already shown several examples on updating values in arrays. Let's look at another.

```
declare(strict_types=1);
function update_array_value(int $subscript, $value)
{

        $customer_record = array (
                array('Pete' ,'Smith' ,'123 Main Street' ,'Atlanta','GA', 30001),
                array('Sally' ,'Parisi' ,'101 South Street' ,'Atlanta' , 'GA' , 30001)
                );

        $customer_record[$subscript] = $value;

}

$temp_array = array('Peter' ,'Smith' , '1234 Main Street' ,'Atlanta', 'GA', 30001);
update_array_value(0, $temp_array);
```

This example totally replaces the *Pete* array with a *Peter* array. 0 is passed into *$subscript* and the *Peter* array is passed into *$value* when the method is called. The method then replaces the contents of position 0 with the values in the *Peter* array. Actually it will also insert the array if the position does not currently exist in the array.

If we just want to change one value in the array, we can make a slight adjustment.

```
declare(strict_types=1);
function update_array_value(int $first_subscript, int $second_subscript, $value)
{

        $customer_record = array (
                array('Pete' ,'Smith' ,'123 Main Street' ,'Atlanta','GA', 30001),
                array('Sally' ,'Parisi' ,'101 South Street' ,'Atlanta' , 'GA' , 30001)
                );

        $customer_record[$first_subscript][$second_subscript] = $value;

}
update_array_value(0, 0, "Peter");
```

This example would replace *Pete* with *Peter*. 0 is passed into *$first_subscript*. 0 is also passed into *$second_subscript*. *Peter* is passed into $value when the method is called. The update method then replaces the contents of position 0,0 with *Peter*. Again, if the position does not exist, it will insert the value into the position.

Let's make a slight change to the Chapter 1 example which combined the ability to insert and update.

If we are using an array with numeric subscript, we can insert into a missing subscript. Also, we can *append* our new values to the end of the array as we have done in several examples.

CHAPTER 3 ▓ MULTIDIMENSIONAL ARRAYS

Example 3-9. update_insert_twodim.php

```php
declare(strict_types=1);

function update_array_value( $value, int $first_subscript = -1, int $second_subscript = -1)
{

        $customer_record = array (
                array('Pete' ,'Smith' ,'123 Main Street' , 'Atlanta','GA', 30001),
                array('Sally' ,'Parisi' ,'101 South Street' , 'Atlanta' , 'GA' , 30001)
                );

        If( $first_subscript != -1 && $second_subscript != -1)
        {

                $customer_record[$first_subscript][$second_subscript] = $value;

        }
        else if ($first_subscript != -1)
        {

                $customer_record[$first_subscript] = $value;

        }
        else
        {

                array_push($customer_record, $value);

        }
}

$temp_array = array('Jackie' ,'Smith' , '123 Main Street' ,'Atlanta','GA', 30001);
update_array_value("770-777-7777", 1, 6);
update_array_value($temp_array, 1);
update_array_value($temp_array);
```

This new version of the update method allows us to insert individual values into any missing positions (or actually replace values from current positions). If both positions are provided (1,6) the method will use both positions to update a value (in this example, the phone number is actually added to the end of the *Sally* array). If only one position is provided, the second position (*$second_subscript*) will default to –1. If the array is two-dimensional (as shown here) an array could be passed to completely replace the existing array (row).

```php
update_array_value($temp_array, 1);
```

The second call to this method will replace the *Sally* array with the *Jackie* array.

```php
update_array_value($temp_array);
```

If no positions are passed, the method will set *$first_subscript and $second_subscript* to –1. This will cause the method to execute the *else* part of the *if* statement, which will use *array_push* to add the array to the end of the existing array.

This update method actually also allows us to also input values in existing positions because the only difference between insert and update is whether there is actually something already in the position.

Every program language has the ability to create arrays for even more dimensions. However, programs become less efficient with each additional dimension. With additional dimensions the operating system must build additional tables in memory to keep track of the location of the data. The logic quickly becomes more complex. It becomes more difficult for humans to relate beyond three or four dimensions (height, width, length, time???). This is why you rarely will see programs that contain arrays with more than three (or four) dimensions.

We have come a long way in a short period of time. Let's take another break and do some practice exercises.

EXERCISES

(You can download all working examples from this chapter at `www.littleoceanwaves.com/arrays/`)

1. Adjust Exercise 1-1 from Chapter 1 to pull book information from a file, create a two-dimensional array from the file, accept information about a book from an html form, add the information to the array, and store the information. Use the code from Example 3-4 or Example 3-5 to help you.

    Before you can read from a file there need to be records in the file. Add the code to save the array into the file first. Then run the program. Verify that the information was saved properly in the file. Then add code to read from the file.

2. Compare the PHP code used in this chapter to create and update two-dimensional arrays to another programming language. Which is easier and more efficient? Why? If you don't have other language examples, search the Web using the language name and arrays, such as the following:

"Creating and updating multidimensional arrays in Java"

CHAPTER 4

▨ ▨ ▨

Associative and Object Arrays

After completing this chapter, the student will be able to...

Define and describe the advantages in using associative arrays

Create a simple PHP associative array

Save values into a simple PHP associative array

Display values contained in simple PHP associative array

Create a multidimensional PHP associative array

Save values into a multidimensional PHP associative array

Display values contained in a multidimensional associative array

Add values from an html form into a multidimensional associative array

Validate values before placing them into an associative array

Define and describe the advantages in using an object array

Create a simple PHP object array

Save values into a simple PHP object array

Add values from an html form into a PHP object array

Display values contain in a simple PHP object array

Validate values before placing them into a simple PHP object array

So far all the examples have included arrays that use numeric subscripts. They are not very descriptive. For example:

```
print customer_record[5];
```

If we ran across this statement in program code, we could determine that the array contains a customer's record. However, what the heck is in position 5? We would not know unless we viewed some actual data in the array itself. PHP allows developers to use alphabetic characters instead of numbers for subscripts.

```
print customer_record['zip_code'];
```

In this example, the subscript is now much more readable. We now know that only zip code information will reside in this area of the array. Arrays that contain alphabetic characters in PHP are commonly called *Associative Arrays*.

© Steve Prettyman 2017
S. Prettyman, *PHP Arrays*, DOI 10.1007/978-1-4842-2556-1_4

Some students get lost when learning about *Associative Arrays*. However, there is no reason to panic. You have already seen them used in every example in this book!!

What?

Yes, remember, it was mentioned in Chapter 1 that **all arrays are the same in PHP**. All arrays are *Associative Arrays*. The only difference between what we discussed before and now is what is placed in the subscript. See Example 4-1:

Example 4-1. process_customer_record.php

```php
<?php
// This program accepts information from example1.html
// This is NOT a complete program. The validate
// methods shown need to be created to clean any input.

$customer_record[0] =
        validate_first_name($_POST['first_name']);
$customer_record[1] =
        validate_last_name($_POST['last_name']);
$customer_record[2] =
        validate_address($_POST['address']);
$customer_record[3] =
        validate_city($_POST['city']);
$customer_record[4] =
        validate_state($_POST['state']);
$customer_record[5] =
        validate_zip_code($_POST['zip_code']);

print "Your name is $customer_record[0] $customer_record[1].";
print " You live at $customer_record[2], $customer_record[3],";
print "$customer_record[4], $customer_record[5]";

?>
```

The subscripts in this example are 0, 1, 2, 3, 4, and 5. That is not very descriptive. Instead, we can use words.

Example 4-2.

```php
<?php
// This program accepts information from example1.html
// This is NOT a complete program.
// The validate methods shown need to be created to clean any input.

$customer_record["first_name"] =
        validate_first_name($_POST['first_name']);
$customer_record["last_name"] =
        validate_last_name($_POST['last_name']);
$customer_record["address"] =
        validate_address($_POST['address']);
$customer_record["city"] =
        validate_city($_POST['city']);
$customer_record["state"] =
        validate_state($_POST['state']);
```

```
$customer_record["zip_code"] =
        validate_zip_code($_POST['zip_code']);

print "Your name is $customer_record['first_name'] $customer_record['last_name']. ";
print "You live at $customer_record['address'], $customer_record['city'],";
print "$customer_record['state'], $customer_record['zip_code']";

?>
```

If we replace each numerical subscript with a more meaningful alphabetic subscript, we produce a program that is much more readable. For example, we see that the *"first_name"* value is accepted from the html form via the *$_POST* method. The value in the property is validated by the *validate_first_name* method. If it is valid, the information is placed into the *$customer_record* array at a location called (you guessed it!) *first_name*. A similar process happens with all the other data retrieved.

▓ **Note**   Notice that the print statement uses single quotes around the subscript name (such as 'first_name') instead of double quotes. You cannot embed double quotes inside of double quotes (which contain the complete string to be printed). You can, in many cases but not all, use single quotes instead.

Let's take a look at another previous example.

Example 4-3. process_customer_array_twodim_saved.php

```
<?php
$customer_file = file_get_contents("customer_data.json");
$customer_record = json_decode($customer_file, TRUE);
$customer = filter_input_array(INPUT_POST);
$customer_info =
        validate_array($customer["customer_record"]);
array_push($customer_record, $customer_info);
print_r($customer_record);
file_put_contents("customer_data.json",json_encode($customer_record));
?>
```

In Example 4-3, a two-dimensional array is retrieved from a file, appended with information from an html form, and saved into the original file. This array used numerical subscripts. We only need to change one line to allow this code to handle an *associative array* that would exist in the *customer_data.json* file.

Example 4-4. process_customer_associate_array_twodim_saved.php

```
<?php
$customer_file = file_get_contents("customer_data.json");
$customer_record = json_decode($customer_file, TRUE);
$customer = filter_input_array(INPUT_POST);
list(
        $customer_info['first_name'],
        $customer_info['last_name'],
        $customer_info['address'],
        $customer_info['city'],
        $customer_info['state'],
```

```
        $customer_info['zip_code']
) = validate_array($customer["customer_record"]);

array_push($customer_record, $customer_info);
print_r($customer_record);
file_put_contents("customer_data.json", json_encode($customer_record));

?>
```

The PHP *list* is a *language construct* that can be used to assign values to multiple properties (variables) at the same time. Before PHP 7, the values were actually assigned in reverse order. PHP 7 assigns them in the order presented. Since we are using actual alphabetic values for our subscripts and not numerical values, the order does not matter.

```
list(
        $customer_info['first_name'],
        $customer_info['last_name'],
        $customer_info['address'],
        $customer_info['city'],
        $customer_info['state'],
        $customer_info['zip_code']
) = validate_array($customer["customer_record"]);
```

This example code would work correctly in either order. The value from position 0 in the *customer_record* array (which came from the html form) will be placed into *$customer_info['first_name']*. The value in position 1 will be placed in *$customer_info['last_name']*. The process would continue for the number of positions in the *customer_record* array.

The number of properties in the list statement should be the same number as the positions in the array. This example should include the previous try/catch blocks shown to capture any errors if there are not as many positions in the array as expected. The try/catch block would also handle any problems with the file itself.

```
Array (
 [0] =>
Array ( [first_name] => default [last_name] => default [address] => default [city] =>
default [state] => default [zip_code] => 10001 )
 [1] =>
 Array ( [zip_code] => 11111 [state] => af [city] => ad [address] => aq [last_name] => as
[first_name] => aa )
)
```

By using *associate arrays* we don't have to worry about the order in which values are saved. In the preceding example, the two arrays are saved in reverse order. However, we access the values by the alphabetic subscript names, not position. *print $customer_record[0]['first_name']* will display the value in that location (*default*) no matter where it actually is located in the array.

Let's look at the changes needed to retrieve and save the information in a MySQL database.

Example 4-5. process_customer_associate_array_twodim_mysqli.php

```
try
{
        $mysqli = new mysqli("localhostorwebsite","userid", "password", "database");
        $query = "SELECT * FROM customers";
        $result = $mysqli->query($query);
        $customer_record = $result->fetch_all(MYSQLI_ASSOC);
        $customer = filter_input_array(INPUT_POST);
        $customer_info = validate_array($customer["customer_record"]);
        array_push($customer_record, $customer_info);
        print_r($customer_record);
        $query = "INSERT INTO customers(first_name, last_name, address, city, state, zip_
        code) VALUES (";
        $query .= $customer_info[first_name'] . "," . $customer_info['last_name'] . ",";
        $query .= $customer_info['address'] . "," . $customer_info['city'] . "," .
        $customer_info['state'] ;
        $query . = "," . $customer_info['zip_code'] . ")";

        $result = $mysqli->query($query);
        $mysqli->close();
}
catch(Exception $e)
{
        // ... no changes in the try blocks
```

Very few changes are needed when handling associative arrays with MySQL.

```
$customer_record = $result->fetch_all(MYSQLI_ASSOC);
```

The *result set identifier* must be changed from returning a numeric array (*MYSQLI_NUM*), as shown in the previous chapter, to return an associative array (*MYSQLI_ASSOC*).

```
$query .= $customer_info[first_name'] . "," . $customer_info['last_name'] . ",";
$query .= $customer_info['address'] . "," . $customer_info['city'] . ",";
$query .= $customer_info['state'] ;
$query . = "," . $customer_info['zip_code'] . ")";
```

The indexes used with each position in the *customer_info* array must also be changed from numeric (0, 1, 2, 3, 4, 5) to alphabetic ('first_name', 'last_name', 'address', 'city', 'state', 'zip_code').

```
$customer_record = array (
        array('Pete' , 'Smith' , '123 Main Street' , 'Atlanta', 'GA', 30001),
        array('Sally' , 'Parisi' , '101 South Street' , 'Atlanta' , 'GA' , 30001)
);
```

We produce the expected results with just two line changes.

```
$query .= $customer_info[first_name'] . "," .$customer_info['last_name'] . ",";
$query .= $customer_info['address'] . "," . $customer_info['city'] . "," ;
$query .= $customer_info['state'] ;
$query . = "," . $customer_info['zip_code'] . ")";
```

61

In Chapter 2 we declared an array and its values using the syntax shown in the preceding. When using the same syntax to declare an *associate array* we must specify the *index* (alphabetic subscript name) and the *value* together.

This is when it can get a little confusing. However, we will keep it as simple as possible.

```
$customer_record = array (
        array(  'first_name' => 'Pete' , 'last_name' => 'Smith' ,
                'address' => '123 Main Street' , 'city' => 'Atlanta',
                'state' => 'GA', 'zip_code' => 30001
        ),
        array(  'first_name' => 'Sally' , 'last_name' => 'Parisi' ,
                'address' => '101 South Street' , 'city' => 'Atlanta' ,
                'state' => 'GA' , 'zip_code' => 30001
        )
);
print_r($customer_record);

Array (
[0] =>
Array ( [first_name] => Pete [last_name] => Smith [address] => 123 Main Street [city] =>
Atlanta [state] => GA [zip_code] => 30001 )
[1] =>
Array ( [first_name] => Sally [last_name] => Parisi [address] => 101 South Street [city] =>
Atlanta [state] => GA [zip_code] => 30001 )
)
```

To add an alphabetic subscript to this example we use the same syntax we discovered in *foreach* loops. *key => value* is used to define each position in the array. The *key* is the subscript name (*'first_name'*). The *value* is the information placed in the location (*'Pete'*).

```
'first_name' => 'Pete'
'last_name' => 'Smith'
'address' => '123 Main Street'
'city' => 'Atlanta'
'state' => 'GA'
'zip_code' => 30001
```

We can then retrieve a value using its subscript name.

```
print $customer_record[0]['last_name'];

Smith

Did you notice that the example did not change the subscript for the rows ([0],[1])?
```

The example did not specify any names for the rows. Remember that all arrays in PHP are the same. There is nothing wrong with mixing numeric and alphabetic subscripts (as shown) in this array.

We can, however, provide a name for our rows if needed.

```
$customer_record = array (

        'first_customer' =>
        array(  'first_name' => 'Pete' , 'last_name' => 'Smith' ,
                'address' => '123 Main Street' ,
                'city' => 'Atlanta', 'state' => 'GA',
                'zip_code' => 30001),

        'second_customer' =>
        array(  'first_name' => 'Sally' , 'last_name' => 'Parisi' ,
                'address' => '101 South Street' ,
                'city' => 'Atlanta' , 'state' => 'GA' , 'zip_code' => 30001)
        );

Array (
        [first_customer] =>
                Array ( [first_name] => Pete
                [last_name] => Smith [address] => 123 Main Street
                [city] => Atlanta [state] => GA [zip_code] => 30001 )
        [second_customer] =>
                Array ( [first_name] => Sally
                [last_name] => Parisi [address] => 101 South Street
                [city] => Atlanta [state] => GA [zip_code] => 30001 ) )
```

To add an alphabetic name to our rows, we, again, use the same *key => value* syntax. The only difference is that the *value* is actually an array (the row).

Example 4-6. foreachassociative.php

```
foreach( $customer_record as $row => $row_array)
{
        foreach( $row_array as $column => $column_value)
        {
                print "Row: $row Column: $column Value: $column_value <br>";
        }

print "<br>";

}

Row: first_customer Column: first_name Value: Pete
Row: first_customer Column: last_name Value: Smith
Row: first_customer Column: address Value: 123 Main Street
Row: first_customer Column: city Value: Atlanta
Row: first_customer Column: state Value: GA
Row: first_customer Column: zip_code Value: 30001
Row: second_customer Column: first_name Value: Sally
Row: second_customer Column: last_name Value: Parisi
Row: second_customer Column: address Value: 101 South Street
Row: second_customer Column: city Value: Atlanta
Row: second_customer Column: state Value: GA
Row: second_customer Column: zip_code Value: 30001
```

There are no changes needed to the *foreach* loops shown previously to display or change values in an associative array.

Why?

Again, all PHP arrays are the same. They have the same logic. Numeric, alphabetic, or a combination of both types of subscripts does not make a major difference in how they are used.

4.1   Deleting

Let's return to one of our examples from Chapter 2.

Example 4-7. deletesubscript2dim.php

```
declare(strict_types=1);
function delete_array_value(int $first_subscript, string $second_subscript)
{

        $customer_record = array (
        array(  'first_name' =>'Pete' ,'last_name' =>'Smith' ,
                'address' =>'123 Main Street' ,'city' => 'Atlanta',
                'state' =>'GA', 'zip_code' =>30001
                ),
        array(  'first_name' =>'Sally' ,'last_name' =>'Parisi' ,
                'address' =>'101 South Street' ,'city' => 'Atlanta' ,
                'state' =>'GA' , 'zip_code' => 30001
                )
        );

        unset($customer_record[$first_subscript][$second_subscript]);
}
delete_array_value(1,'last_name');
```

The same exact logic can be used to remove a value (or row) from an associate array. The only change required is to change the data type accepted into the function from int to string. We could also just remove the data type restrictions and the method would work for any array.

4.1.1   Updating & Inserting

Actually we have already shown several examples on updating values in arrays in the previous chapters. Let's take a quick look at the small amount of changes need to handle associative arrays.

Example 4-8. update-associative.php

```
declare(strict_types=1);
function update_array_value(int $subscript, $value)
{

        $customer_record = array (
                array('first_name' =>'Pete' ,'last_name' =>'Smith',
                'address' =>'123 Main Street' ,'city' => 'Atlanta',
```

```
                    'state' =>'GA', 'zip_code' =>30001),
                array('first_name' =>'Sally' ,'last_name' =>'Parisi' ,
                'address' =>'101 South Street' ,'city' => 'Atlanta' ,
                'state' =>'GA' , 'zip_code' => 30001)
        );

        $customer_record[$subscript] = $value;
}
$temp_array =
        array('first_name' =>'Pete' ,'last_name' =>'Smith' ,
        'address' =>'123 Main Street' ,'city' => 'Atlanta',
        'state' =>'GA', 'zip_code' =>30001);
update_array_value(0, $temp_array);
```

As shown before, this example totally replaces the *Pete* array with a *Peter* array. 0 is still passed into *$subscript* because no name was provided for the arrays that hold records.

Example 4-9. update_associative2.php

```
declare(strict_types=1);

function update_array_value(string $subscript, $value)
{

        $customer_record = array (
        'first_customer' =>
                array( 'first_name' => 'Pete' , 'last_name' => 'Smith' ,
                        'address' => '123 Main Street' ,
                        'city' => 'Atlanta', 'state' => 'GA',
                        'zip_code' => 30001
                ),

        'second_customer' =>
                array( 'first_name' => 'Sally' , 'last_name' => 'Parisi' ,
                        'address' => '101 South Street' ,
                        'city' => 'Atlanta' , 'state' => 'GA' ,
                        'zip_code' => 30001
                )
        );

        $customer_record[$subscript] = $value;
}
$temp_array =
        array( 'first_name' =>'Pete' ,'last_name' =>'Smith' ,
                'address' =>'123 Main Street' ,'city' => 'Atlanta',
                'state' =>'GA', 'zip_code' =>30001
        );
update_array_value('first_customer', $temp_array);
```

If we do name the rows, then, except for the array itself, only one slight change is needed. The data type for the subscript either needs to be changed to string or to be removed altogether. Also, the subscript passed into the function needs to give the name of the array to be replaced.

Both of these examples would replace the array containing *Pete* with the array containing *Peter*. Actually it will also insert the array if the position does not currently exist in the array.

Let's take a look at replacing one value.

Example 4-10. update_associative3.php

```
declare(strict_types=1);
function update_array_value(int $first_subscript, string $second_subscript, $value)
{
$customer_record = array (
        array(  'first_name' =>'Pete' ,'last_name' =>'Smith' ,
                'address' =>'123 Main Street' ,'city' => 'Atlanta',
                'state' =>'GA', 'zip_code' =>30001
        ),
        array(  'first_name' =>'Sally' ,'last_name' =>'Parisi' ,

                'address' =>'101 South Street' ,'city' => 'Atlanta' ,
                'state' =>'GA' , 'zip_code' => 30001
        )
);

        $customer_record[$first_subscript][$second_subscript] = $value;

}

update_array_value(0, 'first_name', "Peter");
```

Only two minor changes (besides the array itself) are needed from the original example from Chapter 2. The data type of the second subscript is changed to string and the string subscript (*first_name*) is passed into the method. As we have seen before, this example would replace *Pete* with *Peter*. Again, if the position does not exist, it will insert the value into the position.

If we are providing alphabetic rows, we only need to change the array, the data type of the first subscript, and the value passed in for the first subscript.

Example 4-11. update_associative4.php

```
declare(strict_types=1);

function update_array_value(string $first_subscript, string $second_subscript, $value)
{

        $customer_record = array (
        'first_customer' =>
                array(  'first_name' => 'Pete' , 'last_name' => 'Smith' ,
                        'address' => '123 Main Street' ,
                        'city' => 'Atlanta', 'state' => 'GA',
                        'zip_code' => 30001
                ),

        'second_customer' =>
                array(  'first_name' => 'Sally' , 'last_name' => 'Parisi' ,
                        'address' => '101 South Street' ,
```

```
                        'city' => 'Atlanta' , 'state' => 'GA' ,
                        'zip_code' => 30001
            )
    );

        $customer_record[$first_subscript][$second_subscript] = $value;

}
update_array_value('first_customer','first_name', "Peter");
```

Let's revisit the method that combines these ideas.

If we are using an array with numeric subscript, we can insert into a missing subscript. Also, we can *append* our new values to the end of the array as we have done in several examples. With associate arrays the actual physical location of the information in the array does not matter since we are referencing our information using alphabetic subscripts.

Example 4-12. insert_update_associative.php

```
declare(strict_types=1);

function update_array_value( $value, string $first_subscript = "none",
                    string $second_subscript = "none")
{

        $customer_record = array (
        array('Pete' ,'Smith' ,'123 Main Street' , 'Atlanta','GA', 30001),
        array('Sally' ,'Parisi' ,'101 South Street' , 'Atlanta' , 'GA' , 30001)
        );

        If( $first_subscript != "none" && $second_subscript != "none")
        {
                $customer_record[$first_subscript][$second_subscript] = $value;
        }
        else if ($first_subscript != "none")
        {
                $customer_record[$first_subscript] = $value;
        }
        else
        {
                array_push($customer_record, $value); }
        }
$temp_array =
        array('Jackie' ,'Smith' , '123 Main Street' ,'Atlanta','GA', 30001);
update_array_value("770-777-7777", "second_customer", "phone_number");
update_array_value($temp_array, "second_customer");
update_array_value($temp_array);
```

As mentioned before, this update method allows us to insert individual values into any missing positions (or actually replace values from current positions). If both positions are provided (*"second_customer", "phone_number"*) the method will use both positions to update a value (in this example, the phone number is actually added with a subscript of *phone_number* to the end of the *Sally* array). If only one

67

position is provided, the second position (*$second_subscript*) will default to *"none."* If the array is two-dimensional (as shown here) an array could be passed to completely replace the existing array (row).

```
update_array_value($temp_array,"second_customer");
```

The second call to this method will replace the *Sally* array with the *Jackie* array.

```
update_array_value($temp_array);
```

If no positions are passed, the method will set $*first_subscript and* $*second_subscript* to *"none."* This will cause the method to execute the *else* part of the *if* statement, which will use *array_push* to add the array to the end of the existing array. A numeric subscript (0) will be created to hold the new row.

This update method actually also allows us to input values in existing positions, because the only difference between insert and update is whether there is actually something already in the position.

Hopefully you can now see that *associative arrays* are a great tool provided by PHP. Code using associative arrays is much more readable. There is also no efficiency difference because all arrays in PHP are stored in memory in the same manner.

4.2   Object Arrays

Let's take a brief look at an *Object Array*. If you are not familiar with *Object-Oriented Programming,* you can skip this section without it causing you any difficulty in Chapter 5.

```php
<?php
class Customer
{
        // all code placed here
}
?>
```

PHP classes are created using the *class* keyword followed by a class name. Class names should be indicated with a capital first letter (*Customer*). All code is then encapsulated (contained) when the {}. If the class is contained in a separate file, the filename should match the class name (*Customer.php*).

```
class Customer
{
        private $first_name = "NFN";
        private $last_name = "NLN";
        private $address = "NA";
        private $city = "NC";
        private $state = "NS";
        private $zip_code = "NZC";
}
```

Properties are protected using the *private* keyword. Each property shown has been given a default value. However, the value will be changed when the user "sets" the property. *Set methods* are used to change property values. *Get methods* are used to retrieve property values.

```php
declare(strict_types=1);
function set_first_name(string $value)
{
        if((strlen($value) > 0) && (strlen($value) < 21))
        {
                $this->first_name = $value;
        }
        else
        {
                throw new Exception("Invalid First Name");
        }
}
```

Using *set methods* allows the ability to verify the data before storage, in a similar manner to the verify methods previously discussed. PHP 7 also allows the ability to restrict the data types accepted into the methods (*int, string, float, bool*), using the *declare* statement and specifying the data type expected.

```php
function set_first_name(string $value)
```

In this example, the function expects a string to be passed into $value from the calling program.

```php
if((strlen($value) > 0) && (strlen($value) < 21))
```

If a string is passed, the method will determine if the value accepted has a length between 1 and 20.

```php
$this->first_name = $value;
```

If the string is between 1 and 20 characters it is saved in the property *first_name*.

```php
What happens if the value is not valid?
```

In this example an exception will be thrown if the value is not a string. However, an exception is not thrown if the length of the string is not 1 to 20 characters. Since a default value (NFN) has been originally placed in the property, that value is retained and the program continues.

```php
declare(strict_types=1);
function get_first_name() : string
{
        return $this->first_name;
}
```

PHP 7 can also restrict the type of data returned from a *get method* using a similar format.

```php
return $this->first_name;                                          .
```

Set methods do not accept values. They only return values. There is no need to a complete a validation of the information that is retrieved from the *first_name* property. The value in the property is assumed to be valid and is retrieved, then passed back to the calling program. If the value in *first_name* is not a string, an exception will be raised.

Example 4-13. objectarrays.php

```php
class Customer
{
        private $first_name = "NFN";
        private $last_name = "NLN";
        private $address = "NA";
        private $city = "NC";
        private $state = "NS";
        private $zip_code = "NZC";

        function __construct( $value1,
                $value2,  $value3,  $value4,
                $value5,  $value6)
        {
                $this->set_first_name($value1);
                $this->set_last_name($value2);
                $this->set_address($value3);
                $this->set_city($value4);
                $this->set_state($value5);
                $this->set_zip_code($value6);
        }

        function set_first_name( $value)
        {
                if((strlen($value) > 0) && (strlen($value) < 16))
                {
                        $this->first_name = $value;
                }
                else
                {
                        throw new Exception("Invalid First Name");
                }
        }

        function set_last_name( $value)
        {
                if((strlen($value) > 0) && (strlen($value) < 21))
                {
                        $this->last_name = $value;
                }
                else
                {
                        throw new Exception("Invalid Last Name");
                }
        }
```

```php
function set_address( $value)
{
        if((strlen($value) > 0) && (strlen($value) < 31))
        {
                $this->address = $value;
        }
        else
        {
                throw new Exception("Invalid Address");
        }
}
function set_city( $value)
{
        if((strlen($value) > 0) && (strlen($value) < 21))
        {
                $this->city = $value;
        }
        else
        {
                throw new Exception("Invalid City");
        }
}
function set_state( $value)
{
        if((strlen($value) > 0) && (strlen($value) < 3))
        {
                $this->state = $value;
        }
        else
        {
                throw new Exception("Invalid State");
        }
}
function set_zip_code( $value)
{
        if(($value >= 11111) && ($value <= 99999))
        {
                $this->zip_code = $value;
        }
        else
        {
                throw new Exception("Invalid Zip Code");
        }
}

function get_first_name()
{ return $this->first_name; }

function get_last_name()
{ return $this->last_name; }
```

```
        function get_address()
        { return $this->address; }

        function get_city()
        { return $this->city; }

        function get_state()
        { return $this->state; }

        function get_zip_code()
        { return $this->zip_code; }

}
```

The preceding class provides a basic structure for storing the customer information.

```
function __construct(string $value1, string $value2, string $value3, string $value4,
string $value5, int $value6)
```

A *constructor method* is shown which accepts all values when the object is created. The constructor passes the values into set methods to validate the data before it is stored. Using this structure an *object array* can be declared to hold all customer objects needed.

We can now pass all information for one customer with just one line of code.

```
$customer_record[] = new Customer("Pete", "Smith",
                "123 Main Street", "Atlanta", "GA", 30001);
```

Position zero of the *customer_record* array would now point to an object holding all of the information for *Pete*.

```
print $customer_record[0]->get_first_name();
Pete
```

Retrieving information from the *object array* just requires calling the correct *get method*.

```
$customer_record[0]->set_first_name('Peter').
```

Changing values just requires calling the correct set method.

If we make a slight change to the *constructor* method shown previously we can pass html data into our object array with very little code.

```
function __construct($value)
{
        $this->set_first_name($value[0]);
        $this->set_last_name($value[1]);
        $this->set_address($value[2]);
        $this->set_city($value[3]);
        $this->set_state($value[4]);
        $this->set_zip_code($value[5]);
}
```

Instead of expecting multiple individual properties passed into the constructor, this version accepts an array and sets the properties based on the positions in the array.

We could also use an associative array by just changing the subscripts ($value['first_name'];).

This new constructor makes passing an html array very easy. We can just change one line from our previous example.

Example 4-14. customer_object.php

```php
<?php
// ... Customer class structure goes here
$customer =filter_input_array(INPUT_POST);

$customer_record[] =
        new Customer($customer["customer_record"]);
var_dump($customer_record);

$customer_record[] = new Customer($customer["customer_record"]);
```

The *customer_record* html array is pulled from the *customer* array, which was populated by values entered by the user in the html form. A *Customer* object is created. The *customer_record* array is passed into the constructor of the *Customer* object.

```php
function __construct($value)
```

The constructor renames the array as *$value.*

```php
set_first_name($value[0]);
set_last_name($value[1]);
set_address($value[2]);
set_city($value[3]);
set_state($value[4]);
set_zip_code($value[5]);
```

The values in each position of the *$value* array are then passed into set methods to populate the new *Customer* object properties. Finally, the *Customer* object is attached to the PHP *$customer_record* array at position 0 (or the next available position).

All of this action takes place because of the one line!

```
array(1)
        { [0]=> object(Customer)#1 (6)
                { ["first_name":"Customer":private]=> string(4) "fred"
                ["last_name":"Customer":private]=> string(5) "smith"
                ["address":"Customer":private]=> string(15) "123 Main Street"
                ["city":"Customer":private]=> string(8) "Marietta"
                ["state":"Customer":private]=> string(2) "GA"
                ["zip_code":"Customer":private]=> string(5) "11111"
        } }
```

In the example, *var_dump* was used, instead of *print_r*, to provide a more detailed view of the array. We can see that the *Customer* object is attached at position 0 of the *customer_record* array with a *first_name* (*"fred"*) and *last_name* (*"smith"*).

There is much more we could discover about *object arrays*. However, the intent is just to get your feet wet. *Why would we use object arrays instead of associative arrays?*

One good example is provided in the gaming industry. In many games, once the user obtains a certain expert level, they are invited to play a bonus round. In order to jump to the bonus round all information related to the current level the user has obtained must be saved. All things on the screen (including the aliens) are objects. These objects can be temporarily saved to an object array while the user plays the bonus round. When the user has completed the round, the objects can be retrieved from the array and placed back into their original positions on the screen. Each object would include properties to indicate their last location to complete this process.

We are already done discussing *Associative and Object Arrays.* As we have seen, only a few coding changes are needed to use associative arrays instead of numerical arrays. Associative arrays allow us to create much more readable code syntax. We no longer need to try to figure out what *$customer_record[0]* contains. We can see that $*customer_record['first_name']* will hold a first name.

Let's try an exercise before Chapter 5.

EXERCISES

(You can download all working examples from this chapter at www.littleoceanwaves.com/arrays/)

1. Adjust Exercise #1 from Chapter 2 to pull book information from a file, create a two-dimensional *Associative Array* from the file, accept information about a book from an html form, add the information to the *Associative Array*, and store the information. Use the code from Example 4-4 to help you.

   Before you can read from a file there needs to be *associative* JSON records in the file. Add the code to save the array into the file first. Then run the program. Verify that the information was saved properly in the file. Then add code to read from the file.

2. What other programming languages have *Associate Arrays?* Give an example of the syntax to create one in another language.

CHAPTER 5

▓ ▓ ▓

PHP Functions—Changing, Splitting, Slicing, and Sorting Arrays

After completing this chapter, the student will be able to...

> Create a simple PHP program which changes the contents of an existing array
>
> Create a simple PHP program which splits an array based on a value or comparison
>
> Create a simple PHP program which slices an array based on a value or comparison
>
> Create a simple PHP program which sorts an array based on a value, comparison, or key

In this chapter we will take a brief look at the PHP functions that are available to change, split, slice, and sort arrays. Many of these functions work with multiple array types (single, multidimensional, and/or associative).

All descriptions of the following functions are provided by the online PHP manual available at www.php.net. Brief examples using each function and a description of the results of these examples are provided. These examples are only meant to get your feet wet. For a more detailed description of the functions shown, and for more examples, visit the online PHP manual.

5.1 Changing Array Contents

array_change_key_case

changes the key to uppercase or lowercase

> *"Returns an array with its keys lower or uppercased, or **FALSE** if array is not an array."*

Syntax:

```
array array_change_key_case ( array $array [, int $case = CASE_LOWER ] )
```

Example:

```
$test_array = array('firstname' => 'Jeff', 'lastname' => 'Smith');
print_r(array_change_key_case($test_array, CASE_UPPER));
```

© Steve Prettyman 2017

S. Prettyman, *PHP Arrays*, DOI 10.1007/978-1-4842-2556-1_5

Output:

```
Array
(
        [FIRSTNAME] => Jeff
        [LASTNAME] => Smith
)
```

In this example, the keys (FIRSTNAME, LASTNAME) are uppercased.

array_fill

fill an array with values

Fills an array with num entries of the value of the value parameter, keys starting at the start_index parameter.

Syntax:

array array_fill (int $start_index , int $num , mixed $value)

First parameter is the starting index. Second parameter is the ending index.

Example:

```
$default_array = array_fill(1, 8, 'default');

print_r($default_array);
```

Output:

```
Array (
        [1] => default
        [2] => default
        [3] => default
        [4] => default
        [5] => default
        [6] => default
        [7] => default
        [8] => default
)
```

In this example, 1 and 8 are passed, providing the starting and ending keys. *Default* is also passed providing the value used to fill the array.

array_fill_keys

fills an array with values, specifying keys

"Fills an array with the value of the value parameter, using the values of the keys array as keys."

Syntax:

array array_fill_keys (array $keys , mixed $value)

Example:

```
$keys = array('first_name', 'last_name', 'address', 'city', 'state', 'zip');
$default_array = array_fill_keys($keys, 'default');
print_r($default_array);
```

76

Output:

```
Array (
        [first_name] => default
        [last_name] => default
        [address] => default
        [city] => default
        [state] => default
        [zip] => default
)
```

In this example, the *$keys* array is used to supply the key. The word '*default*' is used to fill each position.

array_filter

filters elements of an array using a callback function

> *"Iterates over each value in the array passing them to the callback function. If the callback function returns true, the current value from array is returned into the result array. Array keys are preserved."*

This function can be used in several ways to filter out content you don't want in your array.

You can create a function to filter out unwanted data types that exist in the array or use existing PHP functions.

Syntax:

array array_filter (array $array [, callable $callback [, int $flag = 0]])

Example:

```
$first_array = array('first_name' => 'Pete' , 'last_name' => 'Smith' , 'address' => '123
Main Street' , 'city' => 'Atlanta', 'state' => 'GA', 'zip' => 30001);

function filter_array($unfiltered_value)
{
        if(is_string($unfiltered_value))
        {
        return $unfiltered_value;
        }
}

print_r(array_filter($first_array, "filter_array"));
```

Output:

```
Array (
        [first_name] => Pete
        [last_name] => Smith
        [address] => 123 Main Street
        [city] => Atlanta
        [state] => GA
)
```

This example would filter out anything that is not a string.
Without a function, it will filter out empty strings, NULL, or FALSE.

Example:

```
$first_array = array('first_name' => '' , 'last_name' => NULL , 'address' => FALSE , 'city'
=> 'Atlanta', 'state' => 'GA', 'zip' => 30001);

print_r(array_filter($first_array));
```

Output:

```
Array (
        [city] => Atlanta
        [state] => GA
        [zip] => 30001
)
```

A PHP compare function can be used instead of a user-defined function. These could include strcmp, strcasecmp, strncasecmp, substrcomp, or other PHP comparison functions that return < 0, 0, or > 0 as a result.

array_flip

exchanges all keys with their associated values in an array

> *"array_flip() returns an array in flip order, i.e. keys from array become values and values from array become keys."*

Syntax:

array array_flip (array $array)

Example:

```
$first_array = array('first_name' => 'Pete' , 'last_name' => 'Smith' , 'address' => '123
Main Street' , 'city' => 'Atlanta', 'state' => 'GA', 'zip_code' => 30001);

$result = array_flip($first_array);

print_r($result);
```

Output:

```
Array (
        [Pete] => first_name
        [Smith] => last_name
        [123 Main Street] => address
        [Atlanta] => city
        [GA] => state
        [30001] => zip_code
)
```

In this example, the keys and values in array *$first_array* are reversed.

array_pad

pads an array to the specified length with a value

> *"array_pad() returns a copy of the array padded to size specified by size with value value. If size is positive then the array is padded on the right, if it's negative then on the left."*

Syntax:

```
array array_pad ( array $array , int $size , mixed $value )
```

Example:

```
$first_array = array('Pete' , 'Smith' , '123 Main Street' , 'Atlanta', 'GA', '30001');
$second_array = array('Sally' , 'Parisi' , '101 South Street' , 'Atlanta' ,'GA' , '30001');

$first_array = array_pad($first_array, 8, "No Value");
$second_array = array_pad($second_array, -8, "No Value");

print_r($first_array);
print_r($second_array);
```

Output:

```
Array (
        [0] => Pete
        [1] => Smith
        [2] => 123 Main Street
        [3] => Atlanta
        [4] => GA
        [5] => 30001
        [6] => No Value
        [7] => No Value
)

Array (
        [0] => No Value
        [1] => No Value
        [2] => Sally
        [3] => Parisi
        [4] => 101 South Street
        [5] => Atlanta
        [6] => GA
        [7] => 30001
)
```

first_array now has two additional elements at the end of the array. The length of the original array was 6. The padding size entered was 8. Thus, two extra positions are created.

Second_array now has two additional elements at the front of the array. The padding size entered was –8.

array_pop

pops the element off the end of array

> *"array_pop() pops and returns the last value of the array, shortening the array by one element."*

Syntax:

```
mixed array_pop ( array &$array )
```

Example:

```
$first_array = array('Pete' , 'Smith' ,'123 Main Street' , 'Atlanta', 'GA', '30001');

print array_pop($first_array);

print_r($first_array);
```

Output:

```
30001

Array (
        [0] => Pete
        [1] => Smith
        [2] => 123 Main Street
        [3] => Atlanta
        [4] => GA
)
```

The last element of *$first_array* is pulled from the array and displayed via the print statement. The array size is now one less than originally.

array_push

pushes one or more elements onto the end of array

> *"array_push() treats an array as a stack, and pushes the passed variables onto the end of array. The length of array increases by the number of variables pushed."*

Syntax:

```
int array_push ( array &$array , mixed $value1 [, mixed $... ] )
```

Example:

```
$customer_recrod = array (
        array('Pete' , 'Smith' , '123 Main Street' ,'Atlanta', 'GA', 30001),
        array('Sally' , 'Parisi' , '101 South Street' ,'Atlanta' , 'GA' , 30001)
        );

$customer_info = array('Be' , 'Happy' ,'111 North Street' , 'Atlanta' , 'GA' , 30001);
array_push($customer_record, $customer_info);
print_r($customer_record);
```

Output:

```
Array (
[0] =>
Array (
[0] => Pete [1] => Smith [2] => 123 Main Street [3] => Atlanta [4] => GA [5] => 30001
 )
[1] =>
Array (
[0] => Sally [1] => Parisi [2] => 101 South Street [3] => Atlanta [4] => GA [5] => 30001
)
[2] =>
Array (
[0] => Be [1] => Happy [2] => 111 North Street [3] => Atlanta [4] => GA [5] => 30001
)
)
```

array_push adds the *Be Happy* array to the end of the existing array.

array_shift

shifts an element off the beginning of an array

> *"array_shift() shifts the first value of the array off and returns it, shortening the array by one element and moving everything down. All numerical array keys will be modified to start counting from zero while literal keys won't be touched."*

Syntax:

`mixed array_shift ( array &$array )`

Example:

```
$first_array = array('first_name' => 'Pete' ,
                'last_name' => 'Smith' ,
                'address' => '123 Main Street' ,
                'city' => 'Atlanta', 'state' => 'GA',
                'zip_code' => 30001);

$second_array = array('Sally' , 'Parisi' ,'101 South Street' , 'Atlanta' , 'GA' , 30001);

array_shift($first_array);

array_shift($second_array);

print_r($first_array);

print_r($second_array);
```

81

Output:

```
Array (
        [last_name] => Smith
        [address] => 123 Main Street
        [city] => Atlanta [state] => GA
        [zip_code] => 30001
)

Array (
        [0] => Parisi
        [1] => 101 South Street
        [2] => Atlanta
        [3] => GA
        [4] => 30001
  )
```

In *$first_array, first_name* has been removed from the front of the array. In *$second_array, Sally* has been removed and the indexes have been renumbered beginning at 0.

array_unshift

prepends one or more elements to the beginning of an array

> *"array_unshift() prepends passed elements to the front of the array. Note that the list of elements is prepended as a whole, so that the prepended elements stay in the same order. All numerical array keys will be modified to start counting from zero while literal keys won't be touched. "*

Syntax:

```
int array_unshift ( array &$array , mixed $value1 [, mixed $... ] )
```

Example:

```
$first_array = array('Pete' ,'Smith','123 Main Street' ,'Atlanta', 'CA', 30001);
print(array_unshift($first_array, "770-777-7777", "adm@no.co"));
print_r($first_array)
```

Output:

```
8

Array (
        [0] => 770-777-7777
        [1] => adm@no.co
        [2] => Pete
        [3] => Smith
        [4] => 123 Main Street
        [5] => Atlanta
        [6] => CA
        [7] => 30001
)
```

array_unshift will append items to the end of the array. The function will return the new size of the array. In this example, two items are added to the end of *$first_array*.

compact

creates an array containing variables and their values

> *"For each of these, compact() looks for a variable with that name in the current symbol table and adds it to the output array such that the variable name becomes the key and the contents of the variable become the value for that key. In short, it does the opposite of extract().*
>
> *Any strings that are not set will simply be skipped."*

Syntax:

```
array compact ( mixed $varname1 [, mixed $... ] )
```

Example:

```
$first_name = "Pete";
$last_name = "Smith";
$address = "123 Main Street";
$city = "Atlanta";
$state = "GA";
$zip_code = 30001;

$keys = array("first_name", "last_name",
"address", "city", "state", "zip_code");

$first_array = compact($keys);

print_r($first_array);
```

Output:

```
Array (
        [first_name] => Pete
        [last_name] => Smith
        [address] => 123 Main Street
        [city] => Atlanta
        [state] => GA
        [zip_code] => 30001
)
```

compact will build an array from existing variable names that are passed. It will use the variable names for the keys creating an associative array. In this example an array of the variable names is passed, which pulls the values in the variables and creates the array shown. If the variable does not exist, it will ignore it.

range

creates an array containing a range of elements

Syntax:

```
array range ( mixed $start , mixed $end [, number $step = 1 ] )
```

Example:

```
print_r(range(1,10));
```

Output:

```
Array (
        [0] => 1
        [1] => 2
        [2] => 3
        [3] => 4
        [4] => 5
        [5] => 6
        [6] => 7
        [7] => 8
        [8] => 9
        [9] => 10
)
```

range provides a quick way to generate sequential values for an array.

Example:

```
print_r(range('A','F'));
```

Output:

```
Array (
        [0] => A
        [1] => B
        [2] => C
        [3] => D
        [4] => E
        [5] => F
)
```

You are not limited to just numerical values.

Example:

```
print_r(range('F','A'));
```

Output:

```
Array (
        [0] => F
        [1] => E
        [2] => D
        [3] => C
        [4] => B
        [5] => A
)
```

You are also not limited to ascending order.

5.2 Splitting and Slicing Arrays

array_chunk

splits an array into chunks

> *"Chunks an array into arrays with size elements. The last chunk may contain less than size elements."*

Syntax:

array array_chunk (array $array , int $size [, bool $preserve_keys = false])

Example:

```
$test_array = array('Jeff', 'Smith', '123 Main Street', 'Atlanta', 'GA', '30001');
print_r(array_chunk($test_array, 2));
```

Output:

```
Array
(
        [0] => Array
        (
                [0] => Jeff
                [1] => Smith
        )

        [1] => Array
        (
                [0] => 123 Main Street
                [1] => GA
        )

        [2] => Array
        (
                [0] => 30001
        )

)
```

Passing 2 into the function splits the original array into a two-dimensional array with three elements.

Example:

```
$test_array = array('Jeff', 'Smith','123 Main Street', 'Atlanta', 'GA', '30001');
print_r(array_chunk($test_array, 2));
```

Output:

```
Array
(
        [0] => Array
        (
                [0] => Jeff
                [1] => Smith
        )

        [1] => Array
        (
                [2] => 123 Main Street
                [3] => GA
        )

        [2] => Array
        (
                [4] => 30001
        )

)
```

In this example, the original keys (subscripts) are retained within the new two-dimensional array.

array_slice

extracts a slice of the array

> *"array_slice() returns the sequence of elements from the array as specified by the offset and length parameters."*

Syntax:

array array_slice (array $array , int $offset [, int $length = NULL [, bool $preserve_keys = false]])

Example:

```
$second_array = array('Sally' , 'Parisi' ,
 '101 South Street' , 'Atlanta' , 'GA' , 30001);

print_r(array_slice($second_array, 2));
print_r(array_slice($second_array, -2, 1));
print_r(array_slice($second_array, 0, 2));
print_r(array_slice($second_array, 2, -1));
print_r(array_slice($second_array, 2, -1, true));
```

Output:

```
Array (
        [0] => 101 South Street
        [1] => Atlanta
        [2] => GA
        [3] => 30001
)
Array (
        [0] => GA
)
Array (
        [0] => Sally
        [1] => Parisi
 )
Array (
        [0] => 101 South Street
        [1] => Atlanta
        [2] => GA
)
Array (
        [2] => 101 South Street
        [3] => Atlanta
        [4] => GA
)
```

Passing just a 2 will return all values starting at position 2 (*101 South Street, Atlanta, 30001*).

Passing a –2 and 1 will slice from the right instead of left, starting at the second to last right position and return one value (*GA*).

Passing a 0 and 2 will start at position 0 and return two values (*Sally, Parisi*).

Passing a 2 and –1 will start at position 2 and return all items up to the second-to-last right-most item (101 South Street, Atlanta).

Passing 2, –1, and TRUE will return the same as the previous example, except the original indexes are retained.

array_splice

removes a portion of the array and replace it with something else

> *"Removes the elements designated by offset and length from the input array, and replaces them with the elements of the replacement array, if supplied."*

Syntax:

array array_splice (array &$input , int $offset [, int $length = 0 [, mixed $replacement = array()]])

Example:

```
$second_array = array('Sally' , 'Parisi' ,
'101 South Street' , 'Atlanta' , 'GA' , 30001);

print_r(array_splice($second_array, 2));
print_r(array_splice($second_array, 0, 1));
```

Output:

```
Array (
        [0] => 101 South Street
        [1] => Atlanta
        [2] => GA
        [3] => 30001
)
Array (
        [0] => Sally
)
```

In the first example, 2 is passed, which requests that the contents of the array *$second_array* are retained starting at index 2 (the address).

In the second example, 0 and 1 are passed, indicating that starting at position 0, one item should be retained (the first name).

5.3   Sorting Arrays

array_multisort

sorts multiple or multidimensional arrays

> "*array_multisort() can be used to sort several arrays at once, or a multidimensional array by one or more dimensions.*
>
> *Associative (string) keys will be maintained, but numeric keys will be reindexed.*

Sorting type flags:

> ° *SORT_REGULAR - compare items normally (don't change types)*
>
> ° *SORT_NUMERIC - compare items numerically*
>
> ° *SORT_STRING - compare items as strings*
>
> ° *SORT_LOCALE_STRING - compare items as strings, based on the current locale. It uses the locale, which can be changed using setlocale()*
>
> ° *SORT_NATURAL - compare items as strings using "natural ordering" like natsort()*
>
> ° *SORT_FLAG_CASE - can be combined (bitwise OR) with SORT_STRING or SORT_NATURAL to sort strings case-insensitively"*

Syntax:

```
bool array_multisort ( array &$array1 [, mixed $array1_sort_order = SORT_ASC [, mixed
$array1_sort_flags = SORT_REGULAR [, mixed $... ]]] )
```

Example:

```
$first_array = array('Pete' , 'Smith' ,'123 Main Street' , 'Atlanta', 'GA', '30001');
$second_array = array('Sally' , 'Parisi' , '101 South Street' , 'Atlanta' ,'GA' , '30001');

array_multisort($first_array, SORT_ASC,
                $second_array, SORT_DESC );

print_r($first_array);
print_r($second_array);
```

Output:

```
Array (
        [0] => 123 Main Street
        [1] => 30001
        [2] => Atlanta
        [3] => GA
        [4] => Pete
        [5] => Smith
)
Array (
        [0] => 101 South Street
        [1] => 30001
        [2] => Atlanta
        [3] => GA
        [4] => Sally
        [5] => Parisi
)
```

In this example,

> *$first_array* values are sorted as strings in ascending order. String numbers (123, 30001) are first in sorting order followed by 'A', 'G', 'P', and 'S'.

> *$second_array* values are sorted as strings in descending order. String numbers (123, 30001) are first in sorting order followed by 'A', 'G', 'S', and 'P'.

array_reverse

returns an array with elements in reverse order

> *"Takes an input array and returns a new array with the order of the elements reversed."*

Syntax:

array array_reverse (array $array [, bool $preserve_keys = false])

Example:

```
$first_array = array('first_name' => 'Pete' ,
        'last_name' => 'Smith' , 'address' => '123 Main Street' ,
        'city' => 'Atlanta', 'state' =>'GA', 'zip_code' => 30001);
```

```
first_array = array('first_name' => 'Pete' ,
        'last_name' => 'Smith' , 'address' => '123 Main Street' ,

        'city' => 'Atlanta', 'state' =>'GA', 'zip_code' => 30001);

print_r(array_reverse($first_array));
print_r(array_reverse($second_array));
print_r(array_reverse($second_array, TRUE));
```

Output:

```
Array (
        [zip_code] => 30001
        [state] => GA
        [city] => Atlanta
        [address] => 123 Main Street
        [last_name] => Smith
        [first_name] => Pete
)

Array (
        [0] => 30001
        [1] => GA
        [2] => Atlanta
        [3] => 101 South Street
        [4] => Parisi
        [5] => Sally
)

Array (
        [5] => 30001
        [4] => GA
        [3] => Atlanta
        [2] => 101 South Street
        [1] => Parisi
        [0] => Sally
)
```

In this example, the elements in *$first_array* are returned in reverse order. *$second_array* is also returned in reverse order. When passing TRUE in the second parameter, the original numerical indexes are retained.

arsort

sorts an array in reverse order and maintains index association

> *"This function sorts an array such that array indices maintain their correlation with the array elements they are associated with.*
>
> *This is used mainly when sorting associative arrays where the actual element order is significant."*

Syntax:

bool arsort (array &$array [, int $sort_flags = SORT_REGULAR])

Example:

```
$first_array = array('first_name' => 'Pete' , 'last_name' => 'Smith' ,
 'address' => '123 Main Street' , 'city' => 'Atlanta', 'state' => 'CA', 'zip_code' => 30001);

arsort($first_array);

print_r($first_array);
```

Output:

```
Array (
        [zip_code] => 30001
        [last_name] => Smith
        [first_name] => Pete
        [state] => CA
        [city] => Atlanta
        [address] => 123 Main Street
 )
```

arsort is used with associative arrays to sort values. It sorts values in reverse alphabetical order. In this example the ZIP code is listed first because it is numeric. The remaining values are in reverse order. The keys (subscripts) are maintained.

asort

sorts an array and maintain index association

> *"This function sorts an array such that array indices maintain their correlation with the array elements they are associated with. This is used mainly when sorting associative arrays where the actual element order is significant."*

Syntax:

bool asort (array &$array [, int $sort_flags = SORT_REGULAR])

Example:

```
$first_array = array('first_name' => 'Pete' ,
        'last_name' => 'Smith' ,
        'address' => '123 Main Street' ,
        'city' => 'Atlanta',
        'state' => 'CA', 'zip_code' => 30001);

asort($first_array);

print_r($first_array);
```

Output:

```
Array (
        [address] => 123 Main Street
        [city] => Atlanta
        [state] => CA
```

```
        [first_name] => Pete
        [last_name] => Smith
        [zip_code] => 30001
)
```

The function *asort* is used with associative arrays to sort values. It sorts values in alphabetic order. In this example ZIP code is listed last because it is numeric. The remaining values are in alphabetic order. The keys (subscripts) are maintained.

krsort

sorts an array by key in reverse order

> *"Sorts an array by key in reverse order, maintaining key to data correlations. This is useful mainly for associative arrays."*

Syntax:

bool krsort (array &$array [, int $sort_flags = SORT_REGULAR])

Example:

```
$first_array = array('first_name' => 'Pete' , 'last_name' => 'Smith' ,
 'address' => '123 Main Street' , 'city' => 'Atlanta', 'state' => 'CA',
 'zip_code' => 30001);

krsort($first_array);
print_r($first_array);
```

Output:

```
Array (
        [zip_code] => 30001
        [state] => CA
        [last_name] => Smith
        [first_name] => Pete
        [city] => Atlanta
        [address] => 123 Main Street
 )
```

krsort sorts keys in reverse alphabetic order. In this example, *zip_code* is now first in the array, and *address* is last.

ksort

sorts an array by key

> *"Sorts an array by key, maintaining key to data correlations. This is useful mainly for associative arrays."*

Syntax:

bool ksort (array &$array [, int $sort_flags = SORT_REGULAR])

Example:

```
$first_array = array('first_name' => 'Pete' ,
        'last_name' => 'Smith' ,
        'address' => '123 Main Street',
        'city' => 'Atlanta', 'state' => 'CA',
        'zip_code' => 30001);

ksort($first_array);
print_r($first_array);
```

Output:

```
Array (
        [address] => 123 Main Street
        [city] => Atlanta
        [first_name] => Pete
        [last_name] => Smith
        [state] => CA
        [zip_code] => 30001
)
```

ksort sorts array kesy in alphabetic order. In this example, *address* is now first in the array, and *zip_code* is last.

natcasesort

sorts an array using a case-insensitive "natural order" algorithm

> *"This function implements a sort algorithm that orders alphanumeric strings in the way a human being would while maintaining key/value associations. This is described as a "natural ordering"."*

Syntax:

bool natcasesort (array &$array)

Example:

```
$name_array =
array("Pete", "peter", "jones", "Jones");

natcasesort($name_array);

print_r($name_array);
```

Output:

```
Array (
        [3] => Jones
        [2] => jones
        [0] => Pete
        [1] => peter
)
```

natcasesort arranges items in a way that is more natural to humans. In this example all the Jones values appear before any of the Peter values. It ignores case.

natsort

sorts an array using a "natural order" algorithm

> *"This function implements a sort algorithm that orders alphanumeric strings in the way a human being would while maintaining key/value associations. This is described as a "natural ordering"."*

Syntax:

bool natsort (array &$array)

Example:

```
$name_array = array("Pete", "peter",
"jones", "Jones");

natsort($name_array);

print_r($name_array);
```

Output:

```
Array (
        [3] => Jones
        [0] => Pete
        [2] => jones
        [1] => peter
)
```

natsort sorts in a human natural way. However, it does not ignore case. In the preceding example, all uppercase words occur before lowercase. However, notice that the keys (subscripts) are retained, unlike *sort*.

rsort

sorts an array in reverse order

> *"This function sorts an array in reverse order (highest to lowest)."*

Syntax:

```
bool rsort ( array &$array [, int $sort_flags = SORT_REGULAR ] )
```

Example:

```
$first_array = array('first_name' => 'Pete' ,
'last_name' => 'Smith' , 'address' => '123 Main Street' ,
 'city' => 'Atlanta', 'state' => 'CA', 'zip_code' => 30001);

rsort($first_array);

print_r($first_array);
```

Output:

```
Array (
        [0] => 30001
        [1] => Smith
        [2] => Pete
        [3] => CA
        [4] => Atlanta
        [5] => 123 Main Street
)
```

rsort sorts the values in an array in reverse alphabetic order. It does not maintain the keys (subscripts) from the original array. As seen from the example, numerical values would exist first in the sorted array.

shuffle

shuffles an array

> *"This function shuffles (randomizes the order of the elements in) an array."*

Syntax:

bool shuffle (array &$array)

Example:

```
$first_array = array('first_name' => 'Pete' ,
'last_name' => 'Smith' , 'address' => '123 Main Street' ,
 'city' => 'Atlanta', 'state' => 'CA', 'zip_code' => 30001);

shuffle($first_array);

print_r($first_array);
```

Output:

```
Array (
        [0] => CA
        [1] => Pete
        [2] => 123 Main Street
        [3] => 30001
        [4] => Smith
        [5] => Atlanta
)
```

shuffle randomly sorts the order of the values in an array. It does not maintain the keys (subscripts).

sort

sorts an array

> *"This function sorts an array. Elements will be arranged from lowest to highest when this function has completed."*

Syntax:

```
bool sort ( array &$array [, int $sort_flags = SORT_REGULAR ] )
```

Example:

```
$first_array = array('first_name' => 'Pete' ,
 'last_name' => 'Smith' , 'address' => '123 Main Street' ,
 'city' => 'Atlanta', 'state' => 'CA', 'zip_code' => 30001);

sort($first_array);

print_r($first_array);
```

Output:

```
Array (
        [0] => 123 Main Street
        [1] => Atlanta
        [2] => CA
        [3] => Pete
        [4] => Smith
        [5] => 30001
)
```

sort shuffles the array into alphabetic order; it does not maintain the keys (subscripts). String values naturally occur first in the sort order before numerical values as shown in the example.

uasort

sorts an array with a user-defined comparison function and maintain index association

> *"This function sorts an array such that array indices maintain their correlation with the array elements they are associated with, using a user-defined comparison function.*
>
> *This is used mainly when sorting associative arrays where the actual element order is significant."*

Syntax:

bool uasort (array &$array , callable $value_compare_func)

Example:

```
function value_compare($first_value, $second_value)
{
    if ($first_value == $second_value)
        return 0;
    else if ($first_value > $second_value)
        return 1;
    else
        return -1;
}
```

```
$first_array = array('first_name' => 'Pete' ,
 'last_name' => 'Smith' , 'address' => '123 Main Street' ,
 'city' => 'Atlanta', 'state' => 'CA', 'zip_code' => 30001);

uasort($first_array, 'value_compare');

print_r($first_array);
```

Output:

```
Array (
        [address] => 123 Main Street
        [city] => Atlanta
        [state] => CA
        [first_name] => Pete
        [last_name] => Smith
        [zip_code] => 30001
)
```

uasort sorts the array in ascending order of the values in each element as determined by a user-supplied function which evaluates what is equal, greater than, or less than. The keys (subscripts) are maintained from the original array.

The user can modify the comparison shown (such as using === instead of ==) to determine what is "equal." The user-supplied function must return a value < 0, 0, and > 0, as shown in the example function.

```
uasort($first_array, "strcmp");
print_r($first_array);
```

A PHP compare function can be used instead of a user-defined function. These could include strcmp, strcasecmp, strncasecmp, substrcomp, or other PHP comparison functions that return < 0, 0, or > 0 as a result.

uksort

sorts an array by keys using a user-defined comparison function

> *"uksort() will sort the keys of an array using a user-supplied comparison function.*
> *If the array you wish to sort needs to be sorted by some nontrivial criteria, you*
> *should use this function."*

Syntax:

bool uksort (array &$array , callable $key_compare_func)

Example:

```
function key_compare($first_key, $second_key)
{
    if ($first_key == $second_key)
        return 0;
    else if ($first_key > $second_key)
        return 1;
```

```
        else
            return -1;
}

uksort($first_array, "key_compare");
print_r($first_array);
```

Output:

```
Array (
        [address] => 123 Main Street
        [city] => Atlanta
        [first_name] => Pete
        [last_name] => Smith
        [state] => CA
        [zip_code] => 30001
)
```

uksort sorts an array in ascending order by keys (subscripts) based on the comparison provided by a user-supplied function. The function must determine what is equal, what is greater than, and what is less than. The keys (subscripts) from the original array are maintained.

The user can modify the comparison shown (such as using === instead of ==) to determine what is "equal." The user-supplied function must return a value < 0, 0, and > 0, as shown in the example function.

```
uksort($first_array, "strcmp");
print_r($first_array);
```

A PHP compare function can be used instead of a user-defined function. These could include strcmp, strcasecmp, strncasecmp, substrcomp, or other PHP comparison functions that return < 0, 0, or > 0 as a result.

usort

sorts an array by values using a user-defined comparison function

> *"This function will sort an array by its values using a user-supplied comparison function. If the array you wish to sort needs to be sorted by some nontrivial criteria, you should use this function."*

Syntax:

bool usort (array &$array , callable $value_compare_func)

Example:

```
function value_compare($first_value,
 $second_value)
{
    if ($first_value == $second_value)
        return 0;
    else if ($first_value > $second_value)
        return 1;
    else
        return -1;
}
```

```
$first_array = array('first_name' => 'Pete' ,
 'last_name' => 'Smith' , 'address' => '123 Main Street' ,
 'city' => 'Atlanta', 'state' => 'CA', 'zip_code' => 30001);

usort($first_array, 'value_compare');

print_r($first_array);
```

Output:

```
Array (
        [0] => 123 Main Street
        [1] => Atlanta
        [2] => CA
        [3] => Pete
        [4] => Smith
        [5] => 30001
)
```

usort sorts the array in ascending order of the values in each element as determined by a user-supplied function which evaluates what is equal, greater than, or less than. The keys (subscripts) are not maintained from the original array.

The user can modify the comparison shown (such as using === instead of ==) to determine what is "equal." The user-supplied function must return a value < 0, 0, and > 0, as shown in the example function.

```
usort($first_array, "strcmp");
print_r($first_array);
```

A PHP compare function can be used instead of a user-defined function. These could include strcmp, strcasecmp, strncasecmp, substrcomp, or other PHP comparison functions that return < 0, 0, or > 0 as a result.

EXERCISES

1. Create a PHP program containing an array of all the first and last names of the students in your class. Sort the array by last name in alphabetic order. Also sort the array in reverse order.

2. Split the array from #1 into two arrays: one containing first names, the other containing last names.

CHAPTER 6

■ ■ ■

PHP Functions—Comparing and Merging Arrays

After completing this chapter, the student will be able to...

> Create a simple PHP program which compares two arrays on a value, key, or with a user-defined function.

> Create a simple PHP program which merges two arrays via union or intersection

In this chapter we will take a brief look at the PHP functions that compare and merge arrays. Many of these functions work with multiple array types (single, multidimensional, and/or associative).

All descriptions of the following functions are provided by the online PHP manual available at www.php.net. Brief examples using each function and a description of the results of these examples are provided. These examples are only meant to get your feet wet. For a more detailed description of the functions shown, and for more examples, visit the online PHP manual.

6.1   Comparing Arrays

array_diff_assoc

computes the difference of two associative arrays with additional index check

> *"Compares array1 against array2 and returns the difference."*

Syntax:

```
array array_diff_assoc ( array $array1 , array $array2 [, array $... ] )
```

Example:

```
$first_array = array('first_name' => 'Pete' ,
'last_name' => 'Smith' , 'address' => '123 Main Street' ,
'city' => 'Atlanta', 'state' => 'GA', 'zip_code' => 30001);

$second_array = array('first_name' => 'Sally' ,
'last_name' => 'Parisi' , 'address' => '101 South Street' ,
'city' => 'Atlanta' , 'state' => 'GA' , 'zip_code' => 30001);
```

© Steve Prettyman 2017
S. Prettyman, *PHP Arrays*, DOI 10.1007/978-1-4842-2556-1_6

```
$difference = array_diff_assoc($first_array, $second_array);
print_r($difference);
```

Output:

```
Array
(
        [first_name] => Pete
        [last_name] => Smith
        [address] => 123 Main Street
)
```

This example compares $first_array and $second_array. It returns was is different about the first array. If we switch the parameters

Example:

```
$difference = array_diff_assoc($second_array, $first_array);
```

Output:

```
Array
(
        [first_name] => Sally
        [last_name] => Parisi
        [address] => 101 South Street
)
```

This example compares *$first_array* and *$second_array*. It returns was is different about the second array.

array_diff_key

computes the difference of arrays using keys for comparison

> *"Compares the keys from array1 against the keys from array2 and returns the difference."*

Syntax:

array array_diff_key (array $array1 , array $array2 [, array $...])

Example:

```
$first_array = array('first_name' => 'Pete' ,
'last_name' => 'Smith' , 'address' => '123 Main Street' ,
'city' => 'Atlanta', 'state' => 'GA', 'zip' => 30001);

$second_array = array('firstname' => 'Sally' ,
'lastname' => 'Parisi' , 'address' => '101 South Street' ,
'city' => 'Atlanta' , 'state' => 'GA' , 'zipcode' => 30001);

var_dump(array_diff_key($first_array, $second_array));
```

Output:

```
array(3)
 {
        ["first_name"]=> string(4) "Pete"
        ["last_name"]=> string(5) "Smith"
        ["zip"]=> int(30001)
 }
```

This example compares the keys in *$first_array* and *$second_array*. If the keys are different, it returns an array with the keys that are different in the first array.

If we switch parameters

Example:

```
var_dump(array_diff_key($second_array, $first_array));
```

Output:

```
array(3)
{
        ["firstname"]=> string(5) "Sally"
        ["lastname"]=> string(6) "Parisi"
        ["zipcode"]=> int(30001)
}
```

This example compares the keys in $first_array and $second_array. If the keys are different, it returns an array with the keys that are different in the second array.

array_diff_uassoc

computes the difference of arrays with additional index check which is performed by a user-supplied callback function

"Compares array1 against array2 and returns the difference."

Syntax:

array array_diff_uassoc (array $array1 , array $array2 [, array $...], callable $key_compare_func)

Example:

```
$first_array = array('first_name' => 'Pete' ,
'last_name' => 'Smith' , 'address' => '123 Main Street' ,
'city' => 'Atlanta', 'state' => 'GA', 'zip_code' => 30001);

$second_array = array('first_name' => 'Sally' ,
'last_name' => 'Parisi' , 'address' => '101 South Street' ,
'city' => 'Atlanta' , 'state' => 'GA' , 'zip_code' => 30001);

function key_compare($first_value, $second_value)
{
        if ($first_value === $second_value) {
                return 0;
```

```
// if they are the same do return a value
        }
        return ($first_value > $second_value)? 1:-1;
 // if the first value is greater, return that value.
}

print_r( array_diff_uassoc($first_array,
 $second_array, "key_compare"));
```

Output:

```
Array (
        [first_name] => Pete
        [last_name] => Smith
        [address] => 123 Main Street
)
```

In this example, the function *key_compare* causes the values in the first array (*$first_array*) to be returned.

Example:

```
print_r( array_diff_uassoc($second_array, $first_array, "key_compare"));
```

Output:

```
Array (
        [first_name] => Sally
        [last_name] => Parisi
        [address] => 101 South Street
)
```

In this example, the function key_compare causes the values in the first array ($second_array) to be returned.

array_diff_ukey

computes the difference of arrays using a callback function on the keys for comparison

> *"Compares the keys from array1 against the keys from array2 and returns the difference."*

Syntax:

array array_diff_ukey (array $array1 , array $array2 [, array $...], callable $key_ compare_func)

Example:

```
$first_array = array('first_name' => 'Pete' ,
'last_name' => 'Smith' , 'address' => '123 Main Street' ,
'city' => 'Atlanta', 'state' => 'GA', 'zip_code' => 30001);

$second_array = array('firstname' => 'Sally' ,
'lastname' => 'Parisi' , 'address' => '101 South Street' ,
'city' => 'Atlanta' , 'state' => 'GA' , 'zipcode' => 30001);
```

```php
function key_compare($first_value, $second_value)
{
    if ($first_value == $second_value) {
        return 0;
    }
    return ($first_value > $second_value)? 1:-1;
}

var_dump(array_diff_ukey($first_array,
 $second_array, key_compare));
```

Output:

```
array(3) {
        ["first_name"]=> string(4) "Pete"
        ["last_name"]=> string(5) "Smith"
        ["zip_code"]=> int(30001)
}
```

In this example, the function *key_compare* compares the keys and returns the key and value from the first array (*$first_array*), when there is a difference.

Example:

```php
var_dump(array_diff_ukey($second_array, $first_array, 'key_compare'));
```

Output:

```
array(3) {
        ["firstname"]=> string(5) "Sally"
        ["lastname"]=> string(6) "Parisi"
        ["zipcode"]=> int(30001)
}
```

In this example, the function key_compare compares the keys and returns the key and value from the first array (*$second_array*), when there is a difference.

A PHP compare function can be used instead of a user-defined function. These could include strcmp, strcasecmp, strncasecmp, substrcomp, or other PHP comparison functions that return < 0, 0, or > 0 as a result.

array_diff

computes the difference of arrays

> *"Compares array1 against one or more other arrays and returns the values in array1 that are not present in any of the other arrays."*

Syntax:

array array_diff (array $array1 , array $array2 [, array $...])

Example:

```php
$first_array = array("a", "b", "c", "d", "e");
$second_array = array("a", "d", "f", "g", "h");
$difference = array_diff($first_array, $second_array);

print_r($difference);
```

105

Output:

```
Array (
        [1] => b
        [2] => c
        [4] => e
        )
```

In this example, the arrays are compared. If a difference is found, the key and value from the first array (*$first_array*) is returned.

array_udiff_assoc

computes the difference of arrays with additional index check, compares data by a callback function

> *"array_udiff_assoc() returns an array containing all the values from array1 that are not present in any of the other arguments. Note that the keys are used in the comparison unlike array_diff() and array_udiff(). The comparison of arrays' data is performed by using a user-supplied callback."*

Syntax:

array array_udiff_assoc (array $array1 , array $array2 [, array $...], callable $value_compare_func)

Example:

```
$first_array = array('first_name' => 'Pete' ,
'last_name' => 'Smith' , 'address' => '123 Main Street' ,
 'city' => 'Atlanta', 'state' => 'CA', 'zip_code' => 30001);

$second_array = array('firstname' => 'Pete' ,
'last_name' => 'Jones' , 'address' => '123 Main Street' ,
'city' => 'Atlanta', 'state' => 'GA', 'zipcode' => 30001);

function key_compare($first_key, $second_key)
{
    if ($first_key == $second_key)
        return 0;
    else if ($first_key > $second_key)
        return 1;
    else
        return -1;
}

print_r(array_udiff_assoc($first_array,
 $second_array, "key_compare"));
```

Output:

```
Array (
        [first_name] => Pete
        [last_name] => Smith
        [state] => CA
```

```
        [zip_code] => 30001
)
```

In this example, *$first_array* includes a different index (key) for first name than *$second_array*. It also includes a different value in *last_name* and *state*. The ZIP code index (key) is also different.

The user-supplied method causes the indexes (keys) and values from *$first_array* to be returned when there is a difference in either or both the index (key) and value.

A PHP compare function can be used instead of a user-defined function. These could include strcmp, strcasecmp, strncasecmp, substrcomp, or other PHP comparison functions that return < 0, 0, or > 0 as a result.

array_udiff_uassoc

computes the difference of arrays with additional index check, compares data and indexes by a callback function

> *"Returns an array containing all the values from array1 that are not present in any of the other arguments."*

Syntax:

```
array array_udiff_uassoc ( array $array1 , array $array2 [, array $... ], callable $value_
compare_func , callable $key_compare_func )
```

Example:

```
$first_array = array('first_name' => 'Pete' ,
 'last_name' => 'Smith' , 'address' => '123 Main Street' ,
'city' => 'Atlanta', 'state' => 'CA', 'zip_code' => 30001);

$second_array = array('firstname' => 'Pete' ,
 'last_name' => 'Jones' , 'address' => '123 Main Street' ,
'city' => 'Atlanta', 'state' => 'GA', 'zipcode' => 30001);

function key_compare($first_key, $second_key)
{
    if ($first_key == $second_key)
        return 0;
    else if ($first_key > $second_key)
        return 1;
    else
        return -1;
}

function value_compare($first_value,
 $second_value)
{
    if ($first_value == $second_value)
        return 0;
    else if ($first_value > $second_value)
        return 1;
    else
        return -1;
}
```

```
print_r(array_udiff_uassoc($first_array,
        $second_array, "value_compare", "key_compare"));
```

Output:

```
Array (
        [first_name] => Pete
        [last_name] => Smith
        [state] => CA
        [zip_code] => 30001
)
```

The user must supply a function for comparing both the indexes and the values. In this example, both methods use the same logic to make a comparison. If the keys are different, the *first_array* key and value are displayed. If the values are different, the *first_array* key and value are also displayed. Thus, *first_name* is displayed because the indexes are different. *last_name* is displayed because the values are different. *state* is displayed because the values are different. *zip_code* is displayed because the indexes are different.

A PHP compare function can be used instead of a user-defined function. These could include strcmp, strcasecmp, strncasecmp, substrcomp, or other PHP comparison functions that return < 0, 0, or > 0 as a result.

array_udiff

computes the difference of arrays by using a callback function for data comparison

"Returns an array containing all the values of array1 that are not present in any of the other arguments."

Syntax:

array array_udiff (array $array1 , array $array2 [, array $...], callable $value_compare_func)

Example:

```
$first_array = array('first_name' => 'Pete' ,
'last_name' => 'Smith' , 'address' => '123 Main Street' ,
'city' => 'Atlanta', 'state' => 'CA', 'zip_code' => 30001);

$second_array = array('firstname' => 'Pete' ,
'last_name' => 'Jones' , 'address' => '123 Main Street' ,
'city' => 'Atlanta', 'state' => 'GA', 'zipcode' => 30001);

function value_compare($first_value, $second_value)
{
    if ($first_value == $second_value)
        return 0;
    else if ($first_value > $second_value)
        return 1;
    else
        return -1;
}

print_r(array_udiff ($first_array,
$second_array, "value_compare"));
```

Output:

```
Array (
        [last_name] => Smith
        [state] => CA
)
```

User has to supply a function that will compare the values. In this example, if the values are different, the key and value from *$first_array* are displayed. Index differences are ignored. The values in *last_name* and *state* are different in the two arrays.

A PHP compare function can be used instead of a user-defined function. These could include strcmp, strcasecmp, strncasecmp, substrcomp, or other PHP comparison functions that return < 0, 0, or > 0 as a result.

array_uintersect_assoc

computes the intersection of arrays with additional index check, compares data by a callback function

"Returns an array containing all the values of array1 that are present in all the arguments."

Syntax:

array array_uintersect_assoc (array $array1 , array $array2 [, array $...], callable $value_compare_func)

Example:

```
$first_array = array('first_name' => 'Pete' ,
'last_name' => 'Smith' , 'address' => '123 Main Street' ,
 'city' => 'Atlanta', 'state' => 'CA', 'zip_code' => 30001);

$second_array = array('firstname' => 'Pete' ,
'last_name' => 'Jones' , 'address' => '123 Main Street' ,
'city' => 'Atlanta', 'state' => 'GA', 'zipcode' => 30001);

print_r(array_uintersect_assoc($first_array,
$second_array, "strcasecmp"));
```

Output:

```
Array (
        [address] => 123 Main Street
        [city] => Atlanta
)
```

This example is using the PHP method *strcasecmp* to compare strings ignoring the case. If the strings (and the keys) match, the key and index are returned. Only *address* and *city* are matched in both arrays. The programmer can supply a function as shown in other examples. The supplied function must return results <0, 0, and > 0.

Other possible PHP functions that can be used include strcmp, strncasecmp, substrcomp, or any other PHP comparison functions that return < 0, 0, or > 0 as a result.

array_uintersect_uassoc

computes the intersection of arrays with additional index check, compares data and indexes by separate callback functions

> *"Returns an array containing all the values of array1 that are present in all the arguments."*

Syntax:

```
array array_uintersect_uassoc ( array $array1 , array $array2 [, array $... ], callable
$value_compare_func , callable $key_compare_func )
```

Example:

```
$first_array = array('first_name' => 'Pete' ,
'last_name' => 'Smith' , 'address' => '123 Main Street' ,
'city' => 'Atlanta', 'state' => 'CA', 'zip_code' => 30001);

$second_array = array('firstname' => 'Pete' ,
'last_name' => 'Jones' , 'address' => '123 Main Street' ,
'city' => 'Atlanta', 'state' => 'GA', 'zipcode' => 30001);

function key_compare($first_key, $second_key)
{
    if ($first_key == $second_key)
        return 0;
    else if ($first_key > $second_key)
        return 1;
    else
        return -1;
}

function value_compare($first_value, $second_value)
{
    if ($first_value == $second_value)
        return 0;
    else if ($first_value > $second_value)
        return 1;
    else
        return -1;
}

print_r(array_uintersect_uassoc($first_array,
$second_array, "key_compare", "value_compare"));
```

Output:

```
Array (
        [address] => 123 Main Street
        [city] => Atlanta
)
```

This function requires both key and value user-supplied functions. PHP functions could be used (such as *strcascmp*). The user-supplied functions return the key and value if both the key and value are exact matches (except for the case due to == instead of ===). In this example the *address* and *city* are the only matches (for both key and value).

A PHP compare function can be used instead of a user-defined function. These could include strcmp, strcasecmp, strncasecmp, substrcomp, or other PHP comparison functions that return < 0, 0, or > 0 as a result.

array_uintersect

computes the intersection of arrays, compares data by a callback function

> *"Returns an array containing all the values of array1 that are present in all the arguments. "*

Syntax:

```
array array_uintersect ( array $array1 , array $array2 [, array $... ], callable $value_
compare_func )
```

Example:

```
$first_array = array('first_name' => 'Pete' ,
'last_name' => 'Smith' , 'address' => '123 Main Street' ,
'city' => 'Atlanta', 'state' => 'CA', 'zip_code' => 30001);

$second_array = array('firstname' => 'Pete' ,
'last_name' => 'Jones' , 'address' => '123 Main Street' ,
'city' => 'Atlanta', 'state' => 'GA', 'zipcode' => 30001);

function value_compare($first_value, $second_value)
{
    if ($first_value == $second_value)
        return 0;
    else if ($first_value > $second_value)
        return 1;
    else
        return -1;
}

print_r(array_uintersect($first_array,
$second_array, "value_compare"));
```

Output:

```
Array (
        [first_name] => Pete
        [address] => 123 Main Street
        [city] => Atlanta
        [zip_code] => 30001
)
```

This function will ignore differences in the key (subscript). It uses the user-supplied function to compare values. If the values match, the key and value from the first array (*$first_array*) are returned.

In this example, first name, address, city, and ZIP code are returned because they exist in both arrays, even though the keys (subscripts) vary in each array.

The user can modify the comparison shown (such as using === instead of ==) to determine what is "equal." The function must return a value < 0, 0, and > 0.

```
print_r(array_uintersect($first_array, $second_array, "strcmp"));
```

A PHP compare function can be used instead of a user-defined function. These could include strcmp, strcasecmp, strncasecmp, substrcomp, or other PHP comparison functions that return < 0, 0, or > 0 as a result.

6.2   Merging Arrays

array_combine

creates an array by using one array for keys and another for its value

> *"Creates an array using the values from the keys array as keys and the values from the values array as the corresponding values."*

Syntax:

array array_combine (array $keys , array $values)

Example:

```
$first_names = array('Pete', 'Sally', 'Fred');
$last_names = array('Smith', 'Parisi', 'Jones');
$names = array_combine($last_names,
$first_names);
print_r($names);
```

Output:

```
Array
(
        [Smith] => Pete
        [Parisi] => Sally
        [Jones] => Fred
)
```

This example uses the *$last_names* array to populate the keys and the *$first_names* array to populate the values.

array_intersect_assoc

computes the intersection of arrays with additional index check

> *"array_intersect_assoc() returns an array containing all the values of array1 that are present in all the arguments. Note that the keys are used in the comparison unlike in array_intersect()."*

This function compares arrays and returns what is common in both arrays. The index and the value must both be the same.

Syntax:

```
array array_intersect_assoc ( array $array1 , array $array2 [, array $... ] )
```

Example:

```
$first_array = array('first_name' => 'Pete' ,
'last_name' => 'Smith' , 'address' => '123 Main Street' ,
'city' => 'Atlanta', 'state' => 'GA', 'zip_code' => 30001);
$second_array = array('firstname' => 'Sally' ,
'lastname' => 'Parisi' , 'address' => '101 South Street' ,
'city' => 'Atlanta' , 'state' => 'GA' , 'zipcode' => 30001);

$result_array = array_intersect_assoc($first_array, $second_array);

print_r($result_array);
```

Output:

```
Array (
        [city] => Atlanta
        [state] => GA
)
```

Notice that ZIP code was not included because the indexes were not the same. Only *city* and *state* are the same in both arrays.

array_intersect_key

computes the intersection of arrays using keys for comparison

> *"array_intersect_key() returns an array containing all the entries of array1 which have keys that are present in all the arguments."*

Syntax:

```
array array_intersect_key ( array $array1 , array $array2 [, array $... ] )
```

Example:

```
$first_array = array('first_name' => 'Pete' ,
'last_name' => 'Smith' , 'address' => '123 Main Street' ,
'city' => 'Atlanta', 'state' => 'GA', 'zip_code' => 30001);
$second_array = array('firstname' => 'Sally' ,
'lastname' => 'Parisi' , 'address' => '101 South Street' ,
'city' => 'Atlanta' , 'state' => 'GA' , 'zipcode' => 30001);

$result_array = array_intersect_key($first_array,
$second_array);

print_r($result_array);
```

Output:

```
Array (
        [address] => 123 Main Street
        [city] => Atlanta
        [state] => GA
)
```

This function compares keys (only) and returns any key/value pair from the first array that has a matching key in the second array. In this example, even though the values are different in each array, *address, city,* and *state* keys are the same. The values from the first array *($first_array)* are also passed.

array_intersect_uassoc

computes the intersection of arrays with additional index check, compares indexes by a callback function

> *"array_intersect_uassoc() returns an array containing all the values of array1 that are present in all the arguments. Note that the keys are used in the comparison unlike in array_intersect()."*

Syntax:

array array_intersect_uassoc (array $array1 , array $array2 [, array $...], callable $key_compare_func)

Example:

```
$first_array = array('first_name' => 'Pete' ,
 'last_name' => 'Smith' , 'address' => '123 Main Street' ,
 'city' => 'Atlanta', 'state' => 'GA', 'zip_code' => 30001);
$second_array = array('firstname' => 'Sally' ,
 'lastname' => 'Parisi' , 'address' => '101 South Street' ,
 'city' => 'Atlanta' , 'state' => 'GA' , 'zipcode' => 30001);

$result_array = array_intersect_uassoc($first_array,
$second_array, "strcasecmp");

print_r($result_array);
```

Output:

```
Array (
        [city] => Atlanta
        [state] => GA
)
```

This example returns the common values *Atlanta* and *GA* but not the ZIP code since the indexes are different. *strcasecmp* is a PHP function that compares strings. If they are an exact match then this example would return the value as shown (from *$first_array*). Other PHP functions which return 0, >0, or <0 can be used (see next example).

Example:

```
$first_array = array('first_name' => 'Pete' ,
'last_name' => 'Smith' , 'address' => '123 Main Street' ,
 'city' => 'Atlanta', 'state' => 'GA', 'zip_code' => 30001);
$second_array = array('firstname' => 'Sally' ,
 'lastname' => 'Parisi' , 'address' => '101 South Street' ,
 'city' => 'Atlanta' , 'state' => 'GA' , 'zipcode' => 30001);

function key_compare($first_key, $second_key)
{
    if ($first_key == $second_key)
        return 0;
    else if ($first_key > $second_key)
        return 1;
    else
        return -1;
}

$result_array = array_intersect_uassoc($first_array,
$second_array, "key_compare");

print_r($result_array);
```

Output:

```
Array (
        [city] => Atlanta
        [state] => GA
)
```

The programmer can create their own functions. However, they must return 0 (exact match), < 0 (first array is less than second array), or >0 (first array is greater than second array).

Other PHP functions that can be used include strcmp, strcasecmp, substrcomp, or other PHP comparison functions that return < 0, 0, or > 0 as a result.

array_intersect_ukey

computes the intersection of arrays using a callback function on the keys for comparison

> *"array_intersect_ukey() returns an array containing all the values of array1 which have matching keys that are present in all the arguments."*

Syntax:

array array_intersect_ukey (array $array1 , array $array2 [, array $...], callable $key_compare_func)

Example:

```php
$first_array = array('first_name' => 'Pete' ,
'last_name' => 'Smith' , 'address' => '123 Main Street' ,
'city' => 'Atlanta', 'state' => 'GA', 'zip_code' => 30001);
$second_array = array('firstname' => 'Sally' ,
'lastname' => 'Parisi' , 'address' => '101 South Street' ,
 'city' => 'Atlanta' , 'state' => 'GA' , 'zipcode' => 30001);

function key_compare($first_key, $second_key)
{
    if ($first_key == $second_key)
        return 0;
    else if ($first_key > $second_key)
        return 1;
    else
        return -1;
}

$result_array = array_intersect_ukey($first_array,
 $second_array, 'key_compare');

print_r($result_array);
```

Output:

```
Array (
        [address] => 123 Main Street
        [city] => Atlanta
        [state] => GA
)
```

This function ignores the values and only compares keys. Thus, in this example *address* is returned because the keys match even though the values are different. You can use PHP functions (such as *strcasecmp*) instead of your own functions.

A PHP compare function can be used instead of a user-defined function. These could include strcmp, strcasecmp, strncasecmp, substrcomp, or other PHP comparison functions that return < 0, 0, or > 0 as a result.

array_intersect

computes the intersection of arrays

> *"array_intersect() returns an array containing all the values of array1 that are present in all the arguments. Note that keys are preserved."*

Syntax:

array array_intersect (array $array1 , array $array2 [, array $...])

Example:

```php
$first_array = array('first_name' => 'Pete' ,
 'last_name' => 'Smith' , 'address' => '123 Main Street' ,
'city' => 'Atlanta', 'state' => 'GA', 'zip_code' => 30001);
```

```
$second_array = array('firstname' => 'Sally' ,
 'lastname' => 'Parisi' , 'address' => '101 South Street' ,
 'city' => 'Atlanta' , 'state' => 'GA' , 'zipcode' => 30001);

$result_array = array_intersect($first_array,
$second_array);

print_r($result_array);
```

Output:

```
Array (
        [city] => Atlanta
        [state] => GA
        [zip_code] => 30001
)
```

This function compares values and ignores keys. It returns the key that exists in the first array.

array_merge_recursive

merge two or more arrays recursively

> *"array_merge_recursive() merges the elements of one or more arrays together so that the values of one are appended to the end of the previous one. It returns the resulting array.*
>
> *If the input arrays have the same string keys, then the values for these keys are merged together into an array, and this is done recursively, so that if one of the values is an array itself, the function will merge it with a corresponding entry in another array too. If, however, the arrays have the same numeric key, the later value will not overwrite the original value, but will be appended."*

Syntax:

array array_merge_recursive (array $array1 [, array $...])

Example:

```
$first_array = array('first_name' => 'Pete' ,
'last_name' => 'Smith' , 'address' => '123 Main Street' ,
'city' => 'Atlanta', 'state' => 'GA', 'zip_code' => 30001);

$second_array = array('first_name' => 'Sally' ,
'last_name' => 'Parisi' , 'address' => '101 South Street' ,
'city' => 'Atlanta' , 'state' => 'GA' , 'zip_code' => 30001);

$result = array_merge_recursive($first_array,
 $second_array);
print_r($result);
```

Output:

```
Array (
[first_name] => Array
        (       [0] => Pete
```

117

```
                    [1] => Sally
        )
        [last_name] => Array
        (       [0] => Smith
                [1] => Parisi
        )
        [address] => Array
        (
                [0] => 123 Main Street
                [1] => 101 South Street
        )
        [city] => Array
        (       [0] => Atlanta
                [1] => Atlanta
        )
        [state] => Array
        (       [0] => GA
                [1] => GA
        )
        [zip_code] => Array
        (       [0] => 30001
                [1] => 30001
        )
        )
```

Duplicate keys are placed into an array as shown above. This produces a multidimensional array with rows (arrays) of like items, such as *first_name*.

array_merge

merge one or more arrays

"Merges the elements of one or more arrays together so that the values of one are appended to the end of the previous one. It returns the resulting array.

If the input arrays have the same string keys, then the later value for that key will overwrite the previous one. If, however, the arrays contain numeric keys, the later value will not overwrite the original value, but will be appended.

Values in the input array with numeric keys will be renumbered with incrementing keys starting from zero in the result array."

Syntax:

array array_merge (array $array1 [, array $...])

Example:

```
$first_array = array('first_name' => 'Pete' ,
'last_name' => 'Smith' , 'address' => '123 Main Street' ,
'city' => 'Atlanta', 'state' => 'GA', 'zip_code' => 30001);
```

```
$second_array = array('first_name' => 'Sally' ,
'last_name' => 'Parisi' , 'address' => '101 South Street' ,
'city' => 'Atlanta' , 'state' => 'GA' , 'zip_code' => 30001);

$result = array_merge($first_array, $second_array);
print_r($result);
```

Output:

```
Array (
        [first_name] => Sally
        [last_name] => Parisi
        [address] => 101 South Street
        [city] => Atlanta
        [state] => GA
        [zip_code] => 30001
)
```

If the keys are the same in both arrays the second array will dominate as shown above.

Example:

```
$first_array = array('first_name' => 'Pete' ,
'last_name' => 'Smith' , 'address' => '123 Main Street' ,
'city' => 'Atlanta', 'state' => 'GA', 'zip_code' => 30001);

$second_array = array('firstname' => 'Sally' ,
'lastname' => 'Parisi' , 'add' => '101 South Street' ,
'city' => 'Atlanta' , 'st' => 'GA' , 'zipcode' => 30001);

$result = array_merge($first_array, $second_array);
print_r($result);
```

Output:

```
Array (
        [first_name] => Pete
        [last_name] => Smith
        [address] => 123 Main Street
        [city] => Atlanta
        [state] => GA
        [zip_code] => 30001
        [firstname] => Sally
        [lastname] => Parisi
        [add] => 101 South Street
        [cty] => Atlanta
        [st] => GA
        [zipcode] => 30001
)
```

If the indexes are different, the second array will be appended to the first array as shown above.

Example:

```
$first_array = array('Pete' , 'Smith' ,
'123 Main Street' , 'Atlanta', 'GA', 30001);
$second_array = array('Sally' , 'Parisi' ,
'101 South Street' , 'Atlanta' ,'GA' , 30001);

$result = array_merge($first_array, $second_array);
print_r($result);
```

Output:

```
Array (
        [0] => Pete
        [1] => Smith
        [2] => 123 Main Street
        [3] => Atlanta
        [4] => GA
        [5] => 30001
        [6] => Sally
        [7] => Parisi
        [8] => 101 South Street
        [9] => Atlanta
        [10] => GA
        [11] => 30001
)
```

If the arrays are numeric, the keys will be renumbered for the new array created by merging *$first_array* and *$second_array*.

array_replace_recursive

replaces elements from passed arrays into the first array recursively

> *"array_replace_recursive() replaces the values of array1 with the same values from all the following arrays. If a key from the first array exists in the second array, its value will be replaced by the value from the second array. If the key exists in the second array, and not the first, it will be created in the first array. If a key only exists in the first array, it will be left as is. If several arrays are passed for replacement, they will be processed in order, the later array overwriting the previous values."*

Syntax:

array array_replace_recursive (array $array1 , array $array2 [, array $...])

Example:

```
$first_array = array('first_name' => 'Pete' ,
'last_name' => 'Smith' , 'address' => '123 Main Street' ,
'city' => 'Atlanta', 'state' => 'GA', 'zip_code' => 30001);
```

```
$second_array = array('first_name' => 'Sally' ,
'lastname' => 'Parisi' , 'address' => '101 South Street' ,
 'city' => 'Atlanta' , 'state' => 'GA' , 'zipcode' => 30001);

print_r(array_replace_recursive($first_array,
$second_array));
```

Output:

```
Array (
        [first_name] => Sally
        [last_name] => Smith
        [address] => 101 South Street
        [city] => Atlanta
        [state] => GA
        [zip_code] => 30001
        [lastname] => Parisi
        [zipcode] => 30001
)
```

Comparing *$first_array* with *$second_array,* the last name and ZIP code indexes are different. This function will attempt to substitute the values contained in the array in the second parameter (*$second_array*) into the array in the first parameter (*$first_array*). If there is not a related value in the second array (there is no *last_name* or *zip_code*), it will retain the values from the first array. If there are values in the second array that are not in the first array, it will add them to the end of the array (*lastname, zipcode*) produced. This process is recursive.

array_replace

replaces elements from passed arrays into the first array

> *"array_replace() replaces the values of array1 with values having the same keys in each of the following arrays. If a key from the first array exists in the second array, its value will be replaced by the value from the second array. If the key exists in the second array, and not the first, it will be created in the first array. If a key only exists in the first array, it will be left as is. If several arrays are passed for replacement, they will be processed in order, the later arrays overwriting the previous values. "*

Syntax:

array array_replace (array $array1 , array $array2 [, array $...])

Example:

```
$first_array = array('first_name' => 'Pete' ,
'last_name' => 'Smith' , 'address' => '123 Main Street' ,
 'city' => 'Atlanta', 'state' => 'GA', 'zip_code' => 30001);

$second_array = array('first_name' => 'Sally' ,
'lastname' => 'Parisi' , 'address' => '101 South Street' ,
 'city' => 'Atlanta' , 'state' => 'GA' , 'zipcode' => 30001);

print_r(array_replace($first_array, $second_array));
```

Output:

```
Array (
        [first_name] => Sally
        [last_name] => Smith
        [address] => 101 South Street
        [city] => Atlanta
        [state] => GA
        [zip_code] => 30001
        [lastname] => Parisi
        [zipcode] => 30001
)
```

Comparing $first_array with $second_array, the last name and ZIP code indexes are different. This function will attempt to substitute the values contained in the array in the second parameter ($second_array) into the array in the first parameter ($first_array). If there is not a related value in the second array (there is no last_name or zip_code), it will retain the values from the first array. If there are values in the second array that are not in the first array, it will add them to the end of the array (lastname, zipcode) produced. This process is not recursive.

EXERCISES

1. Create a PHP program which contains an array of cities with a population of greater than 100,000 residents in Georgia. Include a second array which contains cities with a population of greater than 100,000 residents in Florida. Using one of the PHP functions shown in this chapter, compare the arrays and display the common elements.

2. Using the arrays from #1, use one of the functions shown in this chapter to merge the arrays without any duplications existing in the new array.

CHAPTER 7

PHP Functions—Searching, Traversing, and Displaying Arrays

After completing this chapter, the student will be able to...

> Create a simple PHP program to search an array for an existing value and/or key
>
> Create a simple PHP program which will traverse through every element of an array without using a loop
>
> Create a simple PHP program which will display contents of an array based on a filter

In this final chapter we will take a brief look at the PHP functions to search, traverse, and display arrays. Many of these functions work with multiple array types (single, multidimensional, and/or associative).

All descriptions of the following functions are provided by the online PHP manual available at www.php.net. Brief examples using each function and a description of the results of these examples are provided. These examples are only meant to get your feet wet. For a more detailed description of the functions shown, and for more examples, visit the online PHP manual.

7.1 Searching Arrays

array_count_values

counts all the values of an array

> *"Returns an array using the values of array as keys and their frequency in array as values."*

Syntax:

```
array array_count_values ( array $array )
```

Example:

```
$silly_array = array("hey", "hey", "hey", "what",
        "is", "this", "unsure", "unsure");
 print_r(array_count_values($silly_array));
```

© Steve Prettyman 2017
S. Prettyman, *PHP Arrays*, DOI 10.1007/978-1-4842-2556-1_7

Output:

```
Array
(
        [hey] => 3
        [what] => 1
        [is] => 1
        [this] => 1
        [unsure] => 2
)
```

This example counts the frequency of the values in *$silly_array*. It creates an array that uses the value as an index and the frequency as the value.

array_column

returns the values from a single column in the input array.

"array_column() returns the values from a single column of the input, identified by the column_key. Optionally, an index_key may be provided to index the values in the returned array by the values from the index_key column of the input array."

Syntax:

array array_column (array $input , mixed $column_key [, mixed $index_key = null])

Example:

```
$customer_record = array (
        array('first_name' => 'Pete' ,
        'last_name' => 'Smith' , 'address' => '123 Main Street' ,
        'city' => 'Atlanta', 'state' => 'GA', 'zip_code' => 30001),
        array('first_name' => 'Sally' ,
        'last_name' => 'Parisi' , 'address' => '101 South Street' ,
        'city' => 'Atlanta' , 'state' => 'GA' , 'zip_code' => 30001)
);

$first_names = array_column($customer_record,
'first_name');
print_r($first_names);
```

Output:

```
Array
(
        [0] => Pete
        [1] => Sally
)
```

In this example, all first names in the *customer_array* are returned.
In PHP 7 you can also specify an index in the second parameter.

Example:

```
$customer_record = array (
        array('first_name' => 'Pete' ,
        'last_name' => 'Smith' ,
         'address' => '123 Main Street' ,
         'city' => 'Atlanta', 'state' => 'GA',
        'zip_code' => 30001),
        array('first_name' => 'Sally' ,
        'last_name' => 'Parisi' ,
         'address' => '101 South Street' ,
         'city' => 'Atlanta' , 'state' => 'GA' ,
        'zip_code' => 30001)
);
$first_names = array_column($customer_record,
 'first_name', 'last_name');
print_r($first_names);
```

Output:

```
Array
(
        [Smith] => Pete
        [Parisi] => Sally
)
```

In this example, the values in *last_name* are used to populate the new keys (subscripts) which are returned from the function.

array_key_exists

checks if the given key or index exists in the array

> *"array_key_exists() returns TRUE if the given key is set in the array. Key can be any value possible for an array index."*

Syntax:

bool array_key_exists (mixed $key , array $array)

Example:

```
$first_array = array('first_name' => 'Pete' ,
'last_name' => 'Smith' , 'address' => '123 Main Street' ,
 'city' => 'Atlanta', 'state' => 'GA', 'zip_code' => 30001);

if (array_key_exists('first_name', $first_array)) {

    print "The 'first_name' is in the array";

}
```

Output:

The 'first_name' is in the array
This function eliminates the need to create a loop when searching for a key in an array.

array_keys

returns all the keys or a subset of the keys of an array

"array_keys() returns the keys, numeric and string, from the array."

Syntax:

array array_keys (array $array [, mixed $search_value = null [, bool $strict = false]])

Example:

```php
$first_array = array('first_name' => 'Pete' ,
 'last_name' => 'Smith' , 'address' => '123 Main Street' ,
'city' => 'Atlanta', 'state' => 'GA', 'zip_code' => 30001);

print_r(array_keys($first_array));
```

Output:

```
Array (
        [0] => first_name
        [1] => last_name
        [2] => address
        [3] => city
        [4] => state
        [5] => zip_code
)
```

This example returns all keys that exist in array *$first_name.*

array_search

searches the array for a given value and returns the corresponding key if successful *"Searches haystack for needle."*

Syntax:

mixed array_search (mixed $needle , array $haystack [, bool $strict = false])

Example:

```php
$first_array = array('first_name' => 'Pete' ,
'last_name' => 'Smith' , 'address' => '123 Main Street' ,
 'city' => 'Atlanta', 'state' => 'GA', 'zip_code' => 30001);

print array_search('123 Main Street', $first_array);
```

Output:

```
address
```

The value passed has to be an exact match. Passing 'Main' only in this example would not return a match.

in_array

checks if a value exists in an array

"Returns TRUE if needle is found in the array, FALSE otherwise."

Syntax:

```
bool in_array ( mixed $needle , array $haystack [, bool $strict = FALSE ] )
```

Example:

```
$first_array = array('first_name' => 'Pete' ,
'last_name' => 'Smith' , 'address' => '123 Main Street' ,
'city' => 'Atlanta', 'state' => 'CA', 'zip_code' => 30001);

if(in_array("Pete",$first_array))
{

        print "Found Pete!";
}

else
{

        print "WE LOST PETE!";

}
```

Output:

```
Found Pete!
```

in_array returns TRUE if the item searched is in the array. It does not return the position of the item in the array. In this example, *Pete* is found in the array.

key_exists

alias of array_key_exists()

"key_exists — Checks if the given key or index exists in the array"

Syntax:

```
bool key_exists ( mixed $key , array $array )
```

Example:

```
$first_array = array('first_name' => 'Pete' ,
 'last_name' => 'Smith' , 'address' => '123 Main Street' ,
 'city' => 'Atlanta', 'state' => 'GA', 'zip_code' => 30001);
```

```
if (key_exists('first_name', $first_array)) {

        print "The 'first_name' is in the array";

}
```

Output:
The Main 'first_name' is in the array
This function eliminates the need to create a loop when searching for a key in an array.

7.2   Traversing Arrays

current

returns the current element in an array

> *"The current() function simply returns the value of the array element that's currently being pointed to by the internal pointer. It does not move the pointer in any way. If the internal pointer points beyond the end of the elements list or the array is empty, current() returns FALSE."*

Syntax:

mixed current (array &$array)

Example:

```
$first_array = array('first_name' => 'Pete' ,
'last_name' => 'Smith' , 'address' => '123 Main Street' ,
 'city' => 'Atlanta', 'state' => 'CA', 'zip_code' => 30001);

print current($first_array) . "<br>";
print next($first_array) . "<br>";
print prev($first_array) . "<br>";
print end($first_array) . "<br>";
```

Output:

```
Pete
Smith
Pete
30001
```

current works with *next, previous,* and *end* to display values located in positions in an array. *current* does not actually move the pointer (position currently accessed) in the array. As shown in this example, only the values are displayed not the keys (subscripts).

each

returns the current key and value pair from an array and advances the array cursor

> *"After each() has executed, the array cursor will be left on the next element of the array, or past the last element if it hits the end of the array. You have to use reset() if you want to traverse the array again using each."*

Syntax:

array each (array &$array)

Example:

```
$first_array = array('first_name' => 'Pete' ,
'last_name' => 'Smith' , 'address' => '123 Main Street' ,
 'city' => 'Atlanta', 'state' => 'CA', 'zip_code' => 30001);

print_r(each($first_array));
print_r(each($first_array));
```

Output:

```
Array (
        [1] => Pete
        [value] => Pete
        [0] => first_name
        [key] => first_name
)

Array (
        [1] => Smith
        [value] => Smith
        [0] => last_name
        [key] => last_name
)
```

each will place the key from the current position in two different elements ([0] and [key]). It will also place the value in two different elements ([1] and [value]). It will also move the cursor (location in the array) to the next element. In this example, the key and value are pulled from the first position of the *$first_name* array. Then the cursor is moved to the next element. The function is called again displaying the information from the second element. The cursor is now positioned at the third element.

end

sets the internal pointer of an array to its last element

> *"end() advances array's internal pointer to the last element, and returns its value."*

Syntax:

mixed end (array &$array)

Example:

```
$first_array = array('first_name' => 'Pete' ,
'last_name' => 'Smith' , 'address' => '123 Main Street' ,
 'city' => 'Atlanta', 'state' => 'CA', 'zip_code' => 30001);

print current($first_array) . "<br>";
print next($first_array) . "<br>";
```

```
print prev($first_array) . "<br>";
print end($first_array) . "<br>";
```

Output:

```
Pete
Smith
Pete
30001
```

In this example, *end* moves the cursor to the last element and returns the value in the element. The ZIP code is displayed.

key

fetches a key from an array

> *"The key() function simply returns the key of the array element that's currently being pointed to by the internal pointer. It does not move the pointer in any way."*

Syntax:

mixed key (array &$array)

Example:

```
$first_array = array('first_name' => 'Pete' ,
'last_name' => 'Smith' , 'address' => '123 Main Street' ,
'city' => 'Atlanta', 'state' => 'CA', 'zip_code' => 30001);

print key($first_array);
```

Output:

```
first_name
```

In this example, the array is currently at the top. *key* will display the key (subscript) at the current position. This function will not move the cursor.

next

advances the internal array pointer of an array

> *"next() behaves like current(), with one difference. It advances the internal array pointer one place forward before returning the element value. That means it returns the next array value and advances the internal array pointer by one."*

Syntax:

mixed next (array &$array)

Example:

```
$first_array = array('first_name' => 'Pete' ,
'last_name' => 'Smith' , 'address' => '123 Main Street' ,
 'city' => 'Atlanta', 'state' => 'CA', 'zip_code' => 30001);

print current($first_array) . "<br>";
print next($first_array) . "<br>";
print prev($first_array) . "<br>";
print end($first_array) . "<br>";
```

Output:

```
Pete
Smith
Pete
30001
```

Next moves to the next element and displays it. In this example *current* displays the first value (*Pete*) but does not advance to the next element. *next* advances to the next element and displays it (*Smith*).

pos

alias of current()

> *"The pos() function simply returns the value of the array element that's currently being pointed to by the internal pointer. It does not move the pointer in any way. If the internal pointer points beyond the end of the elements list or the array is empty, pos() returns FALSE."*

Syntax:

mixed pos (array &$array)

Example:

```
$first_array = array('first_name' => 'Pete' ,
 'last_name' => 'Smith' , 'address' => '123 Main Street' ,
'city' => 'Atlanta', 'state' => 'CA', 'zip_code' => 30001);

print pos($first_array) . "<br>";
print next($first_array) . "<br>";
print prev($first_array) . "<br>";
print end($first_array) . "<br>";
```

Output:

```
Pete
Smith
Pete
30001
```

pos displays the current value but does not move to the next value. In this example *pos* will display *Pete* from the first position but will not move the cursor to the next position. *next* moves to the next position and displays the value (*Smith*).

prev

rewinds the internal array pointer

> *"prev() behaves just like next(), except it rewinds the internal array pointer one place instead of advancing it."*

Syntax:

mixed prev (array &$array)

Example:

```
$first_array = array('first_name' => 'Pete' ,
 'last_name' => 'Smith' , 'address' => '123 Main Street' ,
'city' => 'Atlanta', 'state' => 'CA', 'zip_code' => 30001);

print pos($first_array) . "<br>";
print next($first_array) . "<br>";
print prev($first_array) . "<br>";
print end($first_array) . "<br>";
```

Output:

```
Pete
Smith
Pete
30001
```

In this example, *pos* displays the first value (*Pete*). *next* moves to the next value and displays it (*Smith*). *Prev* moves back a position (back to the first position) and displays the value (*Pete*).

reset

sets the internal pointer of an array to its first element

"reset() rewinds array's internal pointer to the first element and returns the value of the first array element."

Syntax:

mixed reset (array &$array)

Example:

```
$first_array = array('first_name' => 'Pete' ,
 'last_name' => 'Smith' , 'address' => '123 Main Street' ,
'city' => 'Atlanta', 'state' => 'CA', 'zip_code' => 30001);

print pos($first_array) . "<br>";
print next($first_array) . "<br>";
print reset($first_array) . "<br>";
print end($first_array) . "<br>";
```

Output:

```
Pete
Smith
Pete
30001
```

reset moves the pointer to the top of the array. In this example, *pos* returns value in the first element but does not move the pointer. *Next* moves the pointer to the second element and then returns the value store in it. *reset* moves back to the top of the array and returns the value in the first element. *end* is the reverse of *reset*; it moves to the last position of the array and returns the value in that position.

7.3 Displaying Array Contents

array_map

applies the callback to the elements of the given arrays

> "*array_map() returns an array containing all the elements of array1 after applying the callback function to each one. The number of parameters that the callback function accepts should match the number of arrays passed to the array_map()*"

Syntax:

```
array array_map ( callable $callback , array $array1 [, array $... ] )
```

Example:

```
$first_array = array('first_name' => 'Pete' ,
'last_name' => 'Smith' , 'address' => '123 Main Street' ,
 'city' => 'Atlanta', 'state' => 'GA', 'zip_code' => 30001);

function add_info($value)
{
    return("This value is " . $value);
}

print_r(array_map("add_info", $first_array));
```

Output:

```
Array (
        [first_name] => This value is Pete
        [last_name] => This value is Smith
        [address] => This value is 123 Main Street
        [city] => This value is Atlanta
        [state] =>This value is GA
        [zip_code] => This value is 30001
)
```

The function will apply changes to each element, as shown in the function passed (*add_info*), to the array passed to produce a new array with the keys intact. In this example *This value is* is appended to the value of each position in the array to produce a new array.

133

array_product

calculates the product of values in an array

"array_product() returns the product of values in an array."

Syntax:

number array_product (array $array)

Example:

```
$product = array(1, 2, 3, 4, 5, 6, 7, 8, 9, 10);

print array_product($product);
```

Output:

```
3628800
```

In this example will multiply:

```
1 x 2 x 3 x 4 x 5 x 6 x 7 x 8 x 9 x 10 =
362880
```

array_rand

Pick one or more random entries out of an array

"Picks one or more random entries out of an array, and returns the key (or keys) of the random entries."

Syntax:

mixed array_rand (array $array [, int $num = 1])

Example:

```
$first_array = array('Pete' , 'Smith' ,
'123 Main Street' , 'Atlanta', 'GA', '30001');

print_r (array_rand($first_array, 2));
```

Output:

```
Array (
        [0] => 3
        [1] => 5
)
```

In this example *array_rand* picks the third element (*Atlanta*) and the fifth element (*30001*) because two elements were requested.

array_reduce

iteratively reduces the array to a single value using a callback function

> *"array_reduce() applies iteratively the callback function to the elements of the array, so as to reduce the array to a single value."*

Syntax:

```
mixed array_reduce ( array $array , callable $callback [, mixed $initial = NULL ] )
```

Example:

```
$numerical_values =
array(1, 2, 3, 4, 5, 6, 7, 8, 9, 10);

function add($value, $number)
{
    $value += $number;
    return $value;
}

function subtract($value, $number)
{
    $value -= $number;
    return $value;
}
function multiply($value, $number)
{
    $value *= $number;
    return $value;
}

function divide($value, $number)
{
    $value /= $number;
    return $value;
}

print array_reduce($numerical_values,
"add") . "<br>";
print array_reduce($numerical_values,
"subtract") . "<br>";
print array_reduce($numerical_values,
"multiply", -5) . "<br>";; // start with a $value of -5
print array_reduce($numerical_values,
"divide", 5) . "<br>"; //start with a $value of 5
```

Output:

```
55
-55
-18144000
1.3778659611993E-6
```

array_reduce allows you to create your own function to traverse through an array, pick each item, and do something with the item. In these examples, functions are shown to add, subtract, multiply, and divide the items in the array.

```
print array_reduce($numerical_values,
"multiply", -5) . "<br>";; // start with a $value of -5
```

This call starts with an initial value of –5 (which is placed in $value). The result (as seen in the preceding) is a negative value.

```
print array_reduce($numerical_values,
"divide", 5) . "<br>"; //start with a $value of 5
```

This call starts with the 5 being placed into $value before each element value is divided.

array_sum

calculates the sum of values in an array

> *"Returns the sum of values as an integer or float."*

Syntax:

int array_sum(array $array)

Example:

```
$sum = array(1, 2, 3, 4, 5, 6, 7, 8, 9, 10);
```

```
print array_sum($sum);
```

Output:

55

In this example the values in the array are added together.

```
1 + 2 + 3 + 4 + 5 + 6 + 7 + 8 + 9 + 10 = 55
```

array_unique

removes duplicate values from an array

> *"Takes an input array and returns a new array without duplicate values.*
>
> *Note that keys are preserved. array_unique() sorts the values treated as string at first, then will keep the first key encountered for every value, and ignore all following keys. It does not mean that the key of the first related value from the unsorted array will be kept."*

Syntax:

array array_unique (array $array [, int $sort_flags = SORT_STRING])

Example:

```
$first_array = array('first_name' => 'Pete' ,
 'last_name' => 'Smith' , 'address' => '123 Main Street' ,
 'city' => 'Atlanta', 'state' => 'GA', 'zip_code' => 30001,
'first_name' => 'Sally' , 'lastname' => 'Parisi' ,
 'address' => '101 South Street' , 'city' => 'Atlanta' ,
 'state' => 'GA' , 'zipcode' => 30001);

print_r(array_unique($first_array));
```

Output:

```
Array (
        [first_name] => Sally
        [last_name] => Smith
        [address] => 101 South Street
        [city] => Atlanta
        [state] => GA
        [zip_code] => 30001
        [lastname] => Parisi
)
```

This function returns the first unique key for each value. In the example, one occurrence of each key is returned.

array_values

returns all the values of an array

"Returns an indexed array of values."

Syntax:

array array_values (array $array)

Example:

```
$first_array = array('first_name' => 'Pete' , 'last_name' => 'Smith' ,
 'address' => '123 Main Street' , 'city' => 'Atlanta', 'state' => 'CA',
'zip_code' => 30001);

print_r(array_values($first_array));
```

Output:

```
Array (
        [0] => Pete
        [1] => Smith
        [2] => 123 Main Street
        [3] => Atlanta
        [4] => CA
        [5] => 30001
)
```

array_values builds a numerical array of the values in the passed array. It does not retain the keys (subscripts) from the original array.

array_walk_recursive

applies a user function recursively to every member of an array

> *"Applies the user-defined callback function to each element of the array. This function will recurse into deeper arrays."*

Syntax:

```
bool array_walk_recursive ( array &$array , callable $callback [, mixed $userdata = NULL ] )
```

Example:

```
$customer_record = array (
'first_customer' =>

array('first_name' => 'Pete' , 'last_name' => 'Smith' ,
'address' => '123 Main Street' ,
'city' => 'Atlanta', 'state' => 'GA', 'zip_code' => 30001),

'second_customer' =>
array('first_name' => 'Sally' , 'last_name' => 'Parisi' ,
'address' => '101 South Street' ,
'city' => 'Atlanta' , 'state' => 'GA' , 'zip_code' => 30001)
);

function print_customer_info($value, $key)
{
    print " Customer $key is $value<br>";
}

array_walk_recursive($customer_record,
'print_customer_info');
```

Output:

```
Customer first_name is Pete
Customer last_name is Smith
Customer address is 123 Main Street
Customer city is Atlanta
Customer state is GA
Customer zip_code is 30001
Customer first_name is Sally
Customer last_name is Parisi
Customer address is 101 South Street
Customer city is Atlanta
Customer state is GA
Customer zip_code is 30001
```

Array_walk_recursive will apply anything within the programmer-supplied function to each key and value in an array. As seen in this example, this function works well with multidimensional arrays.

138

array_walk

applies a user-supplied function to every member of an array

> *"array_walk() is not affected by the internal array pointer of array. array_walk()*
> *will walk through the entire array regardless of pointer position."*

Syntax:

bool array_walk (array &$array , callable $callback [, mixed $userdata = NULL])

Example:

```
$first_array = array('first_name' => 'Pete' ,
'last_name' => 'Smith' , 'address' => '123 Main Street' ,
 'city' => 'Atlanta', 'state' => 'CA', 'zip_code' => 30001);

function print_customer_info($value, $key)
{
    print " Customer $key is $value<br>";
}

array_walk($first_array, 'print_customer_info');
```

Output:

```
Customer first_name is Pete
Customer last_name is Smith
Customer address is 123 Main Street
Customer city is Atlanta
Customer state is CA
Customer zip_code is 30001
```

Array_walk will apply anything within the programmer-supplied function to each key and value in the array. This function works best with single arrays as shown in the example.

count

counts all elements in an array, or something in an object

> *"Returns the number of elements in array_or_countable. If the parameter is not an*
> *array or not an object with implemented Countable interface, 1 will be returned."*

Syntax:

int count (mixed $array_or_countable [, int $mode = COUNT_NORMAL])

Example:

```
$first_array = array('first_name' => 'Pete' ,
'last_name' => 'Smith' , 'address' => '123 Main Street' ,
'city' => 'Atlanta', 'state' => 'CA', 'zip_code' => 30001);

print count($first_array);
```

Output:

6

count returns the number of elements (size) of the array. In this example, there are six elements. See *sizeof* for another example that can be used with *count*.

extract

imports variables into the current symbol table from an array

Syntax:

```
int extract ( array &$array [, int $flags = EXTR_OVERWRITE [, string $prefix = NULL ]] )
```

Example:

```
$first_array = array('first_name' => 'Pete' ,
'last_name' => 'Smith' , 'address' => '123 Main Street' ,
'city' => 'Atlanta', 'state' => 'CA', 'zip_code' => 30001);

extract($first_array);

print "The first name is " . $first_name . ".
The last name is " . $last_name . ". The address is " .
$address . ". The city is " . $city . ". The state is " . $state .
". The zip is " . $zip_code . ".";
```

Output:

```
The first name is Pete. The last name is Smith. The address is 123 Main Street. The city is
Atlanta. The state is CA. The zip is 30001.
```

This function works with associative arrays. Variables (properties) are created using the key from the array. The values in the array are then placed into the properties. In this example six properties are created using the *extract* function.

sizeof

alias of count()

Syntax:

```
int sizeof ( mixed $array_or_countable [, int $mode = COUNT_NORMAL ] )
```

Example:

```
$first_array = array('Pete' ,'Smith' ,
'123 Main Street' ,'Atlanta', 'CA', 30001);

$count = sizeof($first_array);

for($I=0; $I < $count; $I++)
{

        print $first_array[$I] . "<br />";

}
```

Output:

```
Pete
Smith
123 Main Street
Atlanta
CA
30001
```

sizeof will return the size of the array. Arrays are numbered starting at zero. The last position would be one less than the value returned. Thus, the for loop used in the preceding continues until *$I* is no longer less than the value in *$count*. Notice the example determines the size before the loop, instead of inside the for loop. This provides only one execution of the *sizeof* function instead of calling it seven times in the preceding example. See *count* for another example.

EXERCISES

1. Create a PHP program which contains an array of states in the United States. Use one of the existing functions in this chapter to find any state that begins with "M."

2. Create a PHP program which includes the array from #1; traverse and display the contents of the array without using a loop.

3. Create a PHP program which includes the states and capitals of the United States. Using one of the PHP functions from this chapter, display a message similar to the following for each state:

"The capital of Georgia is Atlanta."

Do not use any loops.

APPENDIX A

■ ■ ■

Case Study—Playing Checkers

In this appendix we will look at the logic in creating a checkers game. The intent is to demonstrate the logical need for an array to accomplish this mission. This example will provide several demonstrations on creating and updating a two-dimensional array. Arrays are commonly used in game development. It is not the intent of this example to provide the complete working code. There are many examples on the Web, if you are interested in the complete solution.

1. What is the first thing we do when we play checkers? Open the box and lay the board out on a table (Figure A-1).

Figure A-1. *Empty checkerboard*

Logically this would map directly to the first logical step in creating a checkers game. A *display_board* function could be designed to show the initial board. Each time the user makes a move, the board will need to be redrawn to indicate a change in what is displayed. The *display_board* function would be called every time the board must be redrawn. Since the location of checkers on the board continuously changes, there needs to be a way to save these changes. As you can see from Figure A-1, the checkerboard has rows and columns just like a two-dimensional array. We can use a two-dimensional array to represent the board and its contents.

The board has eight columns and eight rows. Initially, the red and black colors alternate by column and by row.

© Steve Prettyman 2017
S. Prettyman, *PHP Arrays*, DOI 10.1007/978-1-4842-2556-1

Example A-1. Checkerboard array

```
$checker_board = array (
array ( "black", "red", "black", "red",
"black", "red", "black", "red" ),
array ( "red", "black", "red", "black",
"red" , "black", "red", "black" ),
array ( "black", "red", "black", "red",
"black", "red", "black", "red" ),
array ( "red", "black", "red", "black",
"red" , "black", "red", "black" ),
array ( "black", "red", "black", "red",
"black", "red", "black", "red" ),
array ( "red", "black", "red", "black",
"red" , "black", "red", "black" ),
array ( "black", "red", "black", "red",
"black", "red", "black", "red" ),
array ( "red", "black", "red", "black",
"red" , "black", "red", "black" )
);
```

▓ **Note**   In Figure A-1, the red and black squares are reversed from Figure A-2. The arrays demonstrated are related to the images discussed.

Figure A-2. *Checkerboard with pieces*

Once the array has been created, as shown, the *display_board* function can loop through the array and display the proper board and color combinations using either a series of embedded if statements or a switch statement.

Example A-2. Display board function

```
function display_board() {
foreach( $checker_board as $position) {
switch ($position) {
        case "red" :
        // display a red square or image
                break;
                case "black":
                // display a black square or image
                break;
                default:
                print "Error displaying board";
                break;
        }
}
}
```

The basic structure shown in the preceding will loop through each position in the array, determine the color needed, and then display the color. Since there are many ways that the actual board image could be created, this code it left to the reader to determine. If you are unsure of what to do, check the Internet for suggestions.

2. After the player lays the board on a table, the pieces are then placed in their proper positions (Figure A-2). In an application, this can be done by replacing the positions in the array with the checker pieces.

The programmer could choose to start the game with the pieces already on the board, or require the user to indicate they are ready to play (such as clicking a 'start game') button. We will assume that the player must indicate they want to start a game (or a new game).

A *start_game* function could execute each time the 'start game' button is clicked. This function places the checker pieces in the proper positions by updating the array containing the board, and then calling the *display_board* function to show the board with the checker pieces. As we know, or can see from Figure A-2, all pieces go on the black squares. For the white pieces, the first row pieces are in odd locations, the second row is even (assuming zero if even), and the third row odd again. The red pieces work in reverse.

Example A-3. Start game function

```
function start_game() {
for ($I=0; $I < 8; $I++) {
if( ($I % 2 == 0 )&& ($I != 4 )) {
        for($J=1; $J < 8; $J = $J +2) {
        $checker_board[$I][$j] = ($J == 6) ?
        "red checker" : "white checker";
        }
        }
        else if(($I % 2 !=0) && ($I != 3)) {
        for($J=0; $J < 8; $J = $J + 2) {
        $checker_board[$I][$J] = ($J == 1) ?
```

The outside *for* loop (containing $I) controls the rows. Then initial *if* statement uses $I to determine if the row is even (again assuming that zero is even). If the row is even and not the empty row (4) then the first $J *for* loop is called. This loop starts at column 1 (because a checker is not placed in column 0 on the 0 row) and places a red or white checker in each black square on the board. If it is the sixth row a "red checker" is placed. If it is any other row a "white checker" is placed.

▦ **Suggestion**   Either user a checkerboard or draw a checkerboard on paper and follow along with the logic of these examples.

▦ **Note**   This example does not wipe out any checkers that may be in the "blank" rows. This could be accomplished by coding a loop for the two rows involved and setting each useable position to "black."

The else part of the *if* statement handles the odd-numbered rows. The logic is basically the same except $I starts at 0 instead of 1. Also if the row is 1, then a "white checker" is placed in the position. Otherwise a "red checker" is placed. It skips the third empty row.

After executing the *start_game* function, the array would now contain

Example A-4. Checkerboard array after executing start game function

```
$checker_board = array (
        array ( "red", "white checker", "red",
                "white checker", "red",
                "white checker", "red", "white checker"
        },
        array ( "white checker", "red", "white checker", "red",
                "white checker" , "red", "white checker", "red"
        ),
        array ( "red", "white checker", "red", "white checker",
                "red", "white checker", "red", "white checker"
        },
        array ( "black", "red", "black", "red", "black" ,
                "red", "black", "red"
        ),
        array ( "red", "black", "red", "black", "red",
                "black", "red", "black"
        },
        array ( "red checker", "red", "red checker",
                "red", "red checker" ,
                "red", "red checker", "red"
        ),
        array ( "red", "red checker", "red",
                "red checker", "red", "red checker",
                "red", "red checker"
        },
        array ( "red checker", "red", "red checker",
                "red", "red checker" , "red",
                "red checker", "red"
        )
);
```

We will need to make some changes to the *display_board* function to handle the checkers.

Example A-5. Display board function version 2

```
function display_board() {
foreach( $checker_board as $position) {
switch ($position) {
        case "red" :
        // display a red square or image
        break;
        case "black" :
        // display a black square or image
        break;
        case "white checker" :
        // display a white square or checker image
        break;
        case "red checker" :
        // display a redish square or a checker image
        break;
        default:
        print "Error displaying board";
        break;
        }
}
}
```

We have added *case* procedures to handle the white and red checkers that now exist in the array. When the *start_game* function now calls this *display_board* function, the board will display with the checkers in the proper positions.

3. It is now time for one of our players to move a checker. Let's only be concerned with trying to move a piece, and not all the other factors that may affect our movement. We can always add to a working function after we determine the basic moves.

Top of board

---

start

a   x   **B**

Using the preceding diagram, following the rules of checkers, if we want to move the 'start' white checker (not yet a king), it can only move to position 'a' or 'b'. All other positions are not valid. Notice that position 'a' is one row more than 'start'. Also notice that position 'b' is one more row than 'start'. Thus, part of a valid move is movement only to the next row (we are not concerned with jumps yet). The column of 'a' is one less than the column of 'start'. The column of 'b' is one more than the column of 'start'. This indicates that a valid move is also determined if the column move is one less or one more than the original column. Try this logic and you will discover that this holds true for all moves from the top of the board toward the bottom of the board.

A   x   **B**

start

---

bottom of board

If we want to move a 'start' red checker, it moves in the reverse direction. The valid moves are indicated by positions 'a' and 'b'. Notice that the valid columns, again, are either one more or one less than the column of 'start'. The only difference is that the row will be one less than the row of 'start'. With the white 'start' checker it was one more.

In order to determine valid moves, we will need to collect the original position (row, column) of the checker about to be moved, and the location that the user is attempting to move the checker. Then we will need to make the comparison just described in the last couple of paragraphs.

▦ **Note**   We could do the following collection of information by creating objects for each position in the board. However, to simplify this example, as much as possible, we will use a different technique.

If every black square on the board is a button, and every red square is just an image, we eliminate the worry about the user trying to jump to a red square, or even outside the board itself. We just have to concern ourselves with the restrictions already discussed.

Each black button will actually perform the same code, with one exception; the saving of its location in the $checker_board array.

We can call a function from any of the buttons and pass the location in the array of that button.

```
make_move(3, 3);
```

Each button can pass the row and column of its location in the array into the make_move function. The make_move function will then determine if this is the first click (selecting the checker) or second click (indicating where the checker will move).

Example A-6. Make move function

```
$first_click = false;
$first_row = -1; $first_column = -1;
$second_row = -1; $second_column = -1;
function make_move($row, $column) {
If ($first_click == false) { // first click
        $first_click = true;
        $first_row = $row;
        $first_column = $column;
}
else {
 // second move because $first_click is true
$first_click = false;
 // clears flag even if move is not valid to allow user to try again
$second_row = $row;
$second_column = $column;
valid_move($first_row, $first_column,
 $second_row, $second_column);
}
}
```

The *make_move* function must determine if it is the first click or second click. If it is the first click, the *$first_click* flag is set to true. Then the row and column that were passed into the function are saved into *$first_row* and *$first_column*. That is all that is needed with the first click. If it is a second click, then *$first_click* is set back to false, the values for the row and column are saved in *$second_row* and *$second_column,* and the four row and column values are passed into a *valid_move* function.

Example A-7. Valid move function (if statement)

```
function valid_move($first_row, $first_column,$second_row, $second_column)
{
        If (($checker_board[$first_row][$first_column] ==
                "white checker") &&
                (checker_board[$second_row][$second_column] ==
                "black"))
        {
                If(($second_row - $first_row == 1) &&
                        (($second_column - $first_column == 1) ||
                        ($second_column - $first_column == -1))
                        {$checker_board[$second_row[$second_column] ==
                "white checker";
        $checker_board[$first_row][$first_column] =
                "black";
                        }
```

The *valid_move* function must determine what type of checker we are moving to determine the direction. If it is a white checker, we are moving from top to bottom. It must also make sure that the second clicked area is empty ("black" square). The second row must be one more than the first row. The second column must be one more or one less than the first column. If this is true, the "white checker" is placed in the array at the location of the second click. The position of the first click is changed to be empty ("black" square).

Example A-8. Valid move function (else statement)

```
        } else {
        If ( ($checker_board[$first_row] [$first_column] ==
                "red checker") &&
                ($checker_board[$second_row][$second_column] ==
                "black"))
        {
                If(($second_row - $first_row == -1) &&
                (($second_column - $first_column == 1) ||
                ($second_column - $first_column == -1))
                {
                        $checker_board[$second_row][$second_column] ==
                                "red checker";
                        $checker_board[$first_row] [$first_column] =
                                "black";
                }
        } // if both if statements fail it's not a valid move
        }
display_board();
}
```

If the red checker is moved and the second clicked area is empty ("black" square), the *valid_move* function will determine if the second row selected is one less than the first row. It will also determine if the column is one more or one less than the first column. If this is true, then the "red checker" is moved into the array at the position of the second click. The first click position is set to empty ("black" square).

If any of the following happens, the function will not make a move.

    a.   The first click selected an empty space.

    b.   The second click selected an occupied space.

    c.   The second click did not select a proper square to move.

If a move is not made, the user can try again, because the *$first_click* flag was already set to false. The board is redisplayed (*display_board()*) whether or not a move took place. If it did take place, the *display_board* function will show the changes.

    4.   Let's now consider the process of a checker becoming a "King." This would occur if a red checker reaches row 0 or a white checker reaches row 7. We can add some if statements within our *valid_move* function to determine this situation. Also, kings can move forward or backward. However, they still must follow the other rules.

Example A-9. Valid move function version 2 (if statement)

```
function valid_move($first_row, $first_column,$second_row, $second_column) {
        If (($checker_board[$first_row][$first_column] !=
                "red checker") &&
                (checker_board[$second_row][$second_column] ==
                "black")){
                        If(($second_row - $first_row == 1) &&
                        (($second_column - $first_column == 1) ||
                        ($second_column - $first_column == -1))
                         {
                                If((second_row == 7) &&
                                ($checker_board[$first_row][$first_column] ==
                                        "white checker"))
                                        {
                                        $checker_board[$second_row][$second_column] ==
                                        "white king";
                                        } else {
                                        $checker_board[$second_row][$second_column] ==
                                                $checker_board[$first_row][$first_column];
                                        }
                                $checker_board[$first_row][$first_column] =
                                        "black";
                        }
}
```

Instead of checking for a white checker, white king, or red king to allow movement down the board, it is much shorter code to look for any object that is not a red checker. Only red checkers cannot move down the board. However, when we check for row 7 to determine if we need to crown a checker, we also need to make sure it is a white checker in row 7. We can't crown a red checker, and don't need to crown a white or red king! If we are not crowning a white checker, we are moving either a white checker, a white king, or a red king to a new location. Since we don't know what is moving we can take the value from the first clicked location and copy it into the second clicked location. This will move the proper item.

Example A-10. Valid move function version 2 (else statement)

```
} else {
        If ( ($checker_board[$first_row][$first_column] !=
                "white checker") &&
        ($checker_board[$second_row][$second_column] ==
                "black"))
        {
                If(($second_row - $first_row == -1) &&
                (($second_column - $first_column == 1) ||
                ($second_column - $first_column == -1))
                 {
                        If((second_row == 0) &&
                                ($checker_board[$first_row][$first_column] ==
                                "red checker"))
                        {
                                $checker_board[$second_row][$second_column] ==
                                        "red king";
                        } else {
                                $checker_board[$second_row][$second_column] ==
                                        $checker_board[$fiirst_row][$first_column];
                        } // else
                        $checker_board[$first_row][$first_column] =
                                "black";
                } // end if $second_column - $first_column == -1
        } // not white checker -
        // if both if statements fail it's not a valid move
}
display_board();
}
```

To move up the board, only a white checker is restricted. If a red checker reaches row 0, it is time to become a "red king." Now that we have movement down, we need to make an adjustment to our *display_board* function to allow it to display "red kings" and "white kings."

Example A-11. Display board function version 2

```
function display_board() {
foreach( $checker_board as $position) {
switch ($position) {
        case "red" :
        // display a red square or image
        break;
        case "black" :
        // display a black square or image
        break;
```

```
        case "white checker" :
        // display a white square or checker image
        break;
        case "red checker" :
        // display a redish square or a
        //checker image
        break;
        case "white king" :
        // display a king color square king
        //checker image
        break;
        case "red king" :
        // display a king color square king
        //checker image
        break;
        default:
        print "Error displaying board";
        break;
        }
}
```

As you can see, it only became necessary to add two additional *case* statements for the "white king" and the "red king."

5. Of course, there is no way to win this game unless we can jump the opponent and remove the piece from the board.

```
} // end if $second_column -
    //$first_column == -1
} // not white checker -
//if both if statements fail it's not a valid move
}
display_board();
}
```

In the *valid_move* function, if the flow of the code falls between the last two brackets, it was not a valid move. However, if might be a valid jump.

```
} else  {// not white checker,
    //could it be a jump?
    valid_jump(($first_row, $first_column,$second_row,
                $second_column);
    }
}
display_board();
}
```

Instead of adding more code within the *valid_move* function, it makes sense to instead create a *valid_jump* function and call it if there was not a valid move.

Top of board

		start		
X	ar	X	br	
A	x	W	x	b

Two valid jumps for the white 'start' checker would land the checker on 'a' or 'b'. One additional concern is that a red checker or red king must exist in the 'ar' or 'br' positions or it is not a valid jump. Logically most of this is similar to the move process. Looking at this example, a valid jump for a white checker's row is two more than the original row. The column of a valid jump is two less or two more than the original column. If the checker jumps to 'a', we also need to check the position that is one less row and one more column than position 'a' to make sure a red checker or red king exists. If the checker jumps to 'b', we need to check the position that is one less row and one less column than position 'b' to make sure a red checker or red king exists. If the jump is valid, the 'start' position changes to an empty square, the 'ar' (or 'br') position changes to an empty square, and the 'a' position or 'b' position will now contain the item that did the jumping.

Example A-12. Valid jump function (right side)

```
function valid_jump($first_row,
$first_column,
$second_row, $second_column) {
If (($checker_board[$first_row]
 [$first_column] !=
"red checker") &&
(checker_board[$second_row]
 [$second_column] ==
"black")){
If($second_row - $first_row == 2) {
If($second_column - $first_column == 2) {
        // right side jump attempted
        If((($checker_board[$first_row + 1]
        [$first_column + 1] !=
        "black") &&
        // not jumping empty space
        (substr($checker_board
        [$first_row +1]
         [$first_column + 1],0,3) !=
        Substr($checker_board
        [$first_row] [$first_column],0,3))
        // not jumping its own color
        {
        If((second_row == 7) &&
        ($checker_board[$first_row]
         [$first_column] ==
        "white checker")) {
                $checker_board
        [$second_row] [$second_column] ==
        "white king"; } else {
```

```
        $checker_board[$second_row]
         [$second_column] ==
        $checker_board[$first_row]
        [$first_column]; }
        $checker_board[$first_row]
        [$first_column] == "black";
        $checker_board[$first_row + 1]
        [$first_column + 1] = "black";
        } // end not jump own checker
        //and not jump empty
        } // end right side jump attempted
        else {
        if  ($second_column - $first_column == -2)) {
        // left side jump attempted
                If((($checker_board[$first_row + 1]
                [$first_column - 1] !=
                "black") && // not jumping empty space
        (substr($checker_board[$first_row +1]
        [$first_column - 1],0,3) !=
Substr($checker_board[$first_row]
 [$first_column],0,3))
// not jumping its own color
{
If((second_row == 7) &&
($checker_board[$first_row]
 [$first_column] ==
"white checker"))  {
$checker_board[$second_row]
 [$second_column] ==
"white king"; } else {
$checker_board[$second_row]
[$second_column] ==
$checker_board[$first_row]
 [$first_column]; }
$checker_board[$first_row]
[$first_column)]== "black";
$checker_board[$first_row + 1]
[$first_column - 1] = "black";
} // end not jump own checker and not jump empty
} // end left side jump attempted
} // end jumped two rows
} // end not red and empty place to jump
```

Looking at this half of the required code, the logic (in order) that occurs is

1.   If the checker is not red, it can make a jump down the board. The place it is
      jumping to must also be empty ("black").

2.   If the jump is two rows more than the original position and two columns more
      than the original position, then a right side of the board jump is being attempted.
      (See #7 for left-side jump).

3. If the checker did not jump over an empty ("black") space and the checker did not jump its own kind, then it is a valid jump. The code looks at the first three characters to match "red" or "white" for both the checkers and kings.

4. Did the jumper checker land on row 7? If so, and the checker is white, then make it a king. If not, move the checker from the first position to the second position.

5. Set the first position to empty ("black").

6. Set the position jumped to black.

7. Did the checker jump two columns to the left? If so, it is attempting to jump on the left side of the board.

8. Is the position jumped not empty (not "black") and not the checker's own type, then the jump is valid.

9. Did the jumper checker land on row 7? If so, and the checker is white, then make it a king. If not move the checker from the first position to the second position.

10. Set the first position to empty ("black").

11. Set the position jumped to black.

Example A-13. Valid jump function (left side)

```
else {
If (($checker_board[$first_row] [$first_column] !=
"white checker") &&
(checker_board[$second_row]
 [$second_column] ==
"black")){
        If($second_row - $first_row == -2) {
        If($second_column - $first_column == 2) {
        // right side jump attempted
If((($checker_board[$first_row - 1]
[$first_column + 1] !=
"black") && // not jumping empty space
(substr($checker_board[$first_row - 1]
 [$first_column + 1],0,3) !=
Substr($checker_board[$first_row]
[$first_column],0,3))
// not jumping its own color
{
If((second_row == 0) &&
($checker_board[$first_row]
 [$first_column] ==
"red checker"))  {
        $checker_board[$second_row]
 [$second_column] ==
"red king"; } else {
$checker_board[$second_row]
[$second_column] ==
$checker_board[$first_row]
 [$first_column]; }
```

```
$checker_board[$first_row]
[$first_column] == "black";
$checker_board[$first_row - 1]
 $first_column + 1] = "black";
} // end not jump own checker
// and not jump empty
} // end right side jump attempted
else {
if  ($second_column - $first_column == -2)) {
// left side jump attempted
If((($checker_board[$first_row - 1]
[$first_column - 1] !=
"black") && // not jumping empty space
(substr($checker_board[$first_row -1]
[$first_column - 1],0,3) !=
Substr($checker_board[$first_row]
[$first_column],0,3))
// not jumping its own color
{
If((second_row == 0) &&
($checker_board[$first_row]
 [$first_column] ==
"white checker"))  {
$checker_board[$second_row]
[$second_column] ==
"white king"; } else {
$checker_board[$second_row]
[$second_column] ==
$checker_board[$first_row]
 [$first_column]; }
$checker_board[$first_row]
[$first_column] == "black";
$checker_board[$first_row - 1]
 [$first_column - 1] = "black";
} // end not jump own checker and not jump empty
} // end left side jump attempted
} // end jumped two rows
} // end not white and empty place to jump
```

The else part of the main if statement handles the jumping from the bottom of the board toward the top of the board. The logic is the same except for minor changes. The second row must be two less than the first row (instead of two more). The changes required are highlighted.

There are no requirements to change in the *display_board* function to handle jumps because all changes occur in how items are positioned in the array. There are no new items in the array.

A stated at the beginning of this appendix, the goal of these examples is to show the necessity of arrays, especially in the gaming industry. There are more efficient ways to design this type of application with object arrays and recursion. However, these techniques are beyond the scope of this book.

To complete the coding of a checkers game, additional code would be required to enforce the following rules and techniques.

1. A scoring ability must keep track of the number of checkers and be reduced each time a checker is removed from the board. A player wins when all the other opponents' checkers are removed. However, a player also wins when the opponent cannot make any other moves. This would require the program to look at all possible moves a player can accomplish. A technique to keep track of the number of wins for each player is needed.

2. A technique to keep players from trying to move when it is not their turn is necessary.

3. Depending on the version of checkers, some versions do not allow checker pieces to jump kings. Some versions do not allow checker pieces to jump at all. The code shown does allow checker pieces to jump kings.

4. A recursion technique is needed to allow multiple jumps in the same turn. Depending on the version of checkers, players may be required to jump if they can. This would require coding to determine all possible jumps after the player selects a piece to move.

Index

© Steve Prettyman 2017
S. Prettyman, *PHP Arrays*, DOI 10.1007/978-1-4842-2556-1

▓ S

▓ T, U, V, W, X, Y, Z

Get the eBook for only $4.99!

Why limit yourself?

Now you can take the weightless companion with you wherever you go and access your content on your PC, phone, tablet, or reader.

Since you've purchased this print book, we are happy to offer you the eBook for just $4.99.

Convenient and fully searchable, the PDF version enables you to easily find and copy code—or perform examples by quickly toggling between instructions and applications.

To learn more, go to http://www.apress.com/us/shop/companion or contact support@apress.com.

Printed in the United States
By Bookmasters